D0291137

Strange But True Newfoundland Stories

by
Jack Fitzgerald

Strange But True Newfoundland Stories

by
Jack Fitzgerald

Creative Publishers
P.O. Box 967
St. John's, Newfoundland, Canada   A1C 5M3
1989

© 1989, Jack Fitzgerald

The publisher acknowledges the financial contribution of the *Department of Tourism and Culture, Government of Newfoundland and Labrador,* which has helped make this publication possible.

Appreciation is expressed to *The Canada Council* for publication assistance.

1st printing April 1989
2nd printing December 1992
3rd printing April 1996

∝ Printed on acid-free paper

Published by
CREATIVE BOOK PUBLISHING
a division of 10366 Newfoundland Limited
a Robinson-Blackmore Printing & Publishing associated company
P.O. Box 8660, St. John's, Newfoundland A1B 3T7

Printed in Canada by:
ROBINSON-BLACKMORE PRINTING & PUBLISHING

Canadian Cataloguing in Publication Data

Fitzgerald, Jack, 1945-

   Strange but true Newfoundland stories

   ISBN 0-920021-57-3

1. Newfoundland — History.
2. Legends — Newfoundland.   I. Title

FC2161.8.F58   1989   971.8   C89-098566-9
F1122.6F58   1989

Dedicated to my son Maurice, his step-sister
Christine Sawka and my grand-niece Megan Peach.

Special Thanks to Richard (Dick) Hartery for assistance with
researching material for this book; to the staff of the Provincial Archives for their usual kindness and cooperation; to Am-
brose Cahill for help in out of town visits and arranging
photographs; to Dr. Bobbie Robertson and the Newfoundland
Historical Society for allowing me access to their treasure of
Newfoundland materials; and a special thanks to former Premier Joseph R. Smallwood for his encouragement and
cooperation.

CONTENTS

Chapter 1
Ghost Stories

Captain Bob Bartlett of Brigus gained world fame as an Arctic explorer. He was once asked by a reporter if he believed in ghosts, and his answer probably sums up the feelings most people have on the existence of ghosts. Bartlett answered, "Well, sometimes I do, and sometimes I don't." He added that he had many experiences with the supernatural that made him believe in ghosts, even though he didn't want to believe.

One such instance involved the wreck of the *Falcon*. Bartlett's Uncle Harry was Captain of the *Falcon* when it set out in 1894 from Philadelphia with a cargo of coal to St. John's. A few days later a neighbour of the Bartlett's at Brigus ran into Bob's house to announce incredibly that she had seen Harry Smith, a crewmember on the *Falcon*, in his window as she walked past his house. Mrs. Bartlett told the neighbour that this was impossible because the Falcon wasn't due to arrive in Newfoundland for another week. The neighbour insisted that she had seen the spirit of Harry Smith; she felt sure that the *Falcon* was lost at sea and all hands were dead. Several days later word was received at Brigus that the *Falcon* had been lost at sea — and all hands were dead. This represents one of the occasions on which the famous Captain Bob believed in ghosts.

Another such happening involved the wreck of the *Gertrude*. Under the command of Captain Thomas Carew, the *Gertrude* left St. John's one day to pick up sealing crews along the Southern Shore. The ship disappeared somewhere along the Shore and her fate was a mystery. Then one day, a brother of one of the crewmen of the *Gertrude*, while hunting in the woods, saw a man sitting on a rock. He felt strange as he neared the figure and recognized it as his brother. He asked, "Did you make Renews Rock?" (A rock outside Renews Harbour). The apparition answered, "How true, how true," and disappeared. Eventually the wreck of the *Gertrude* was discovered on the bottom near Renews Rock.

Foran's Hotel Ghost — Every community in Newfoundland has its ghost stories. One of the many handed down in the St. John's area involves the old Foran's Hotel in downtown St. John's. The hotel at one time was actually shunned by local people for more than a month because they believed it to be haunted. Foran's Hotel was located on the site now occupied by the General Post Office on Water Street.

During one dark cold winter night guests at the hotel were awakened by a loud knocking. They gathered in the hallway puzzling over the knocking that continued. Two men left the group and conducted a search of the hotel. They traced the sound to an upstairs room. Upon entering, the noise suddenly stopped. Although the men thoroughly searched the room, they could find no explanation for the noise.

The knocking would resume each night and always end when someone entered the vacant room. Word of the strange happening spread and people began staying away from the hotel. Eventually the haunting faded out and customers began to return. Six month's later a stranger registered. He was escorted to the haunted room by a staff member who found humour in the fact that they finally had a guest for the room.

At midnight a sudden thunderous knocking erupted and people rushed to the hallways to see what was happening. When the hotel manager made his way to the haunted room and opened the door, the knocking stopped . . . . but lying on the floor was the stranger, with a look of terror on his face. When the undertaker went into the room to remove the body the knocking broke out again, and lasted about a minute. The stranger was buried at the cemetery on Waterford Bridge Road — and the knocking in the hotel room stopped forever.

Ghosts at St. Shott's — One of the worst sea disasters to take place at St. Mary's Bay was the wreck of the *Harpooner*, a British troop ship carrying soldiers and their families home to England. The ship, with more than 200 people on board, was lost during a stormy night near St. Shott's. Tradition in the area claims that some of the marines who managed to get safely to shore were buried alive under a portion of cliff when it gave way after being weakened by the wild seas. That tradition is kept alive through the naming of the place — 'Marine's Cove' — in their memory.

Many years passed without any strange happenings. Then one night a fishing boat anchored in the cove. Its crew had no idea of the history of Marine's Cove. During the night, the man on watch sighted a long boat towing another, each loaded to the gunwales with men, women and children.

A big man with strong features was steering. As it passed under the counter of the fishing boat, the helmsman called up to the lookout, "What's our course to round Cape English?" "Nor, Nor-east," the lookout answered. He then went below to tell the Captain he had just seen a shipwrecked crew. The other fishermen followed him on deck just in time to see the boat's lantern fading shoreward.

This photo of a peaceful St. Shott's Beach makes it hard to comprehend the violent storm that caused the wreck of the *Harpooner*. (Photo-Jack Fitzgerald)

Early next morning, with a heavy gale blowing, the fishermen searched the coastline for signs of the wreck or the survivors. There was no sign of any survivors nor evidence of any shipwreck. When they told their story to residents of a nearby village, they were informed that they had seen the ghosts of the marines lost in the *Harpooner* disaster of many years before.

A Mother's Love — John Mallory, who was born around the year 1880 in a Conception Bay community then called Silver Beach, passed away in St. John's during 1952. Throughout his lifetime John fascinated friends and strangers with an account of a supernatural event in his life, which up to his dying day he insisted was absolute truth.

John was the only son of Jake Mallory and Mary Sheldon. A strong love bound the family together, but this happy family-life came to an abrupt end when John was just three years old, his mother passed away. A little over a year later his father took a new bride; however, she resented young John because he was a constant reminder of Mary Sheldon, Jake's first wife.

Sarah, John's step-mother, showed her disapproval by demanding that Jake remodel the house which Mary had designed and Jake had built. She was also very unkind towards her stepson. Although his father was loving and kind to him, he usually spent a lot of time away from home, fishing.

As soon as John grew big enough to do chores around the house, Sarah put him to work. If he delayed in the performance of these chores at all, she would complain to his father. This hurt John more than if she had beaten him, because John loved his father very much. When John reached the age of 12, Sarah began sending him into the woods for firewood.

Once this took place in mid-November, a miserable day with freezing rain. If Jake had been home, he would not have sent John into the woods under such conditions. When he arrived home after dark and learned that John had not returned he immediately raised an alarm throughout the community and a search party was formed. They searched throughout the night as temperatures dropped and the freezing rain increased. Daylight came and passed and still there was no sign of young John.

Near mid-day, while searching a heavily wooded area, Jake

4

came face to face with his son. While embracing him and saying a quiet prayer of thanks, Jake noticed that John was dry and warm, and there was nothing visible to show he had spent a harsh fall night in the outdoors.

When asked for an explanation, John said that he had wandered through the woods crying out for help. When darkness set in, he came across a house with a light in the window. A woman came to the door and beckoned him to come inside. He spent the night there and left at daylight. He spoke of how kind the lady was and how safe and warm he felt in her presence. But Jake knew there was no such house in the forest, and he asked John to describe the woman and the house.

The house described by the boy was exactly like Jake's house as it existed before John's mother passed away. The lady described by John was identical to his mother, who had died nearly 10 years before.

St. Mary's Keys — An act of kindness by Con Sullivan at St. Mary's during the winter of 1863 lead to a supernatural occurance at sea that saved the lives of Sullivan and his crew. It had been a hard winter at St. Mary's. There had been a poor fishery and wild game was scarce. Winter was drawing to an end and families were running short of food and supplies. One evening during this period when Sullivan was playing cards with some friends, a neighbour named Mat Cooney entered the house crying, "God save all here." It was Ash Wednesday. Cooney had a wife and eight children and his winter supply of food had run out. He pleaded with Con to ". . . spare a pan of flour. I haven't got a crumb left."

Con Sullivan, interupting his card game, stood up and said, "Well, Mat by, I am on the last barrel of flour and half of it is yours."

The winter passed and the fishing season finally arrived. On May 1st Sullvian took his five-man crew to the fishing ground at Cape St. Mary's. At the mouth of St. Mary's Bay there is a breaker identified on maps as the Keys. Many ships had crashed upon the keys and many lives were lost there.

After three weeks fishing, Sullivan's crew had taken a full load of fish and were returning to home port. Suddenly a dense fog moved in, followed by nightfall. It was impossible to see. At 2:30 a.m. Tom Fewer was coming on deck with a mug of tea for the Captain. He recalled, "As I looked I saw the form of another man standing by the skipper. I could feel the hair rise on the back of my neck. All the crew were in bed, and the Captain alone was on deck. It was a misty form that stood near him. As I looked I heard a shout . . . 'The Keys, the keys! — ard down, for God's sake! ard down! The skipper acted quickly and spun the wheel. We narrowly escaped hitting the keys. When I looked at the Captain, the misty figure had disappeared. The captain turned to me and said, "Well, by I was well paid for the half barrel of flour I gave Mat Cooney last Ash Wednesday. He came and stood by me and let a screach out of him — the keys, the keys! ard down, for God's sake! ard down.' "

When Sullivan's little fishing vessel arrived at St. Mary's, they learned that Nat Cooney had passed away at 2:30 a.m. that same morning. Before he died he puzzled friends and relatives sitting with him when he suddenly jumped up and shouted," The Key's, the Key's!" Then he lay back and died.

The Haunted Cove — Old-timers along the Southern Shore of Newfoundland say there is a fascinating tale of a haunted cove near St. Shott's. The strange happenings there are said to be connected with an incident and an individual who lived at St. Shott's about 150 years ago.

The individual was a mysterious Englishman. He kept to himself and acted strangely when people came near him. The old-timers say he always behaved suspiciously. They referrred to him as "the wrecker." They felt he deliberately lured vessels to destruction upon the shores, then looted them. But then fate took a hand.

One night a tremendous storm with heavy gale-force winds struck along the Southern Shore. The storm was one of the worst to hit the area in years and people stayed indoors. The next day, after the storm had ended, local fishermen discovered that the wreckage of a vessel had washed ashore during the storm. Amid the rubble they found the body of a lovely young woman. They also found "the Wrecker" himself wandering around in a state of shock. Questioning and investigation by the fishermen determined that during the storm the old man had used a lantern to lure the vessel onto the beach and disaster. When "the Wrecker" went to loot the vessel, he disco-

6

vered the body of the girl and immediately recognized her. He went into shock. The dead girl was the daughter of a woman he had courted in his youth but who turned down his offer of marriage. He then came to Newfoundland and took up the life of a hermit at St. Shott's.

Old-timers still swear that before bad weather breaks the spirit of the dead girl with the spirit of "the Wrecker" kneeling beside her in tears appear on the beach at St. Shott's.

The Ghost of Alice — The diary of Aaron Thomas, preserved at the Newfoundland archives, describes the area between Springdale Street and Flower Hill (during the 19th century) as being the most beautiful natural flower garden in the world. That area was later used as a race track and the local gentry spent many an enjoyable evening there. It was also the site haunted for a decade by the spirit of Alice Janes, who was among the city's most ardent racing enthusiasts. With her Irish-knit shawl and jug of brew, Alice was a fixture at the race track.

During one of the many races there, Alice suffered a sudden heart-attack and died instantly. The whole town turned out for the funeral and she was given a respectable send off at the old cemetery adjoining the Anglican Cathedral.

A year passed. On the anniversary of Alice's death a young woman was being escorted through the Flower Hill field by a male companion. Darkness was just beginning to set in and the girl complained of a strange cold feeling. She asked her friend to take her home. As they neared the edge of the field they came upon a sight that sent them screaming from the area. They later described the apparition that had frightened them. At first it seemed like an old woman sitting on a rock holding a jug in her hand. When the couple neared the figure, it slowly stood up and stared straight at them. Her eyes were burning red and her white hair stood out like the whisks of a broom.

The couple recognized the figure as the spirit of Alice Janes. When word of the apparition spread throughout town, several friends of the late Alice Janes visited the race track and then the gravesite to pray. While at the graveside they noticed that the tombstone which had marked the grave had disappeared. They searched the graveyard, but were unable to find it.

The apparition was reportedly seen on the anniversary of

Alice's death for about a decade. Then one day the caretaker at the cemetery, while clearing an area of the graveyard, found the missing tombstone. He placed it back on the gravesite. The apparations ceased, and Alice's spirit was never heard from again.

Devil's Hand — Fortune Harbour is a small community in Notre Dame Bay. In its early days it was a thriving fishing community, and men from all over Europe settled there. Among them was a man called Kincheler. The game of 45's was a popular one in that community and Kincheler was an expert player. Neither distance nor harsh weather would deter him from seeking out a game of cards. In fact, every night he would walk three miles just to play 45's.

One such night he walked the three miles from Fortune Harbour to Webber's Bight to play a game. The others in the game kidded him about his zeal for playing cards, and one gentleman suggested that Kincheler would play cards with anyone, anywhere and at anytime. Kincheler's response to this was, "Yes, I'd have a game of cards with the devil himself." Everyone had a great laugh at this. Sometime after midnight the game ended and Kincheler left Webber's Bight to return home.

It was a beautiful moonlit night. During his walk he met a stranger who stopped him to ask where he was going so late at night. Kincheler replied that he was returning home from a card game, adding that there was nothing he loved more than a game of cards. The stranger said he shared the same interest and challenged Kincheler to a game. Kincheler agreed, and the two card-enthusiasts moved to a large flat rock nearby which they used as a card table.

The card game went well until the last hand, with Kincheler in sight of winning the game. The stranger was obviously upset over the possibility of losing. It was then that Kinchella noticed the twitching tail extending from behind the stranger.

Kincheler was more interested in winning the game than in the strange appearance of his visitor. He triumphantly played his final card, beating the card played by the stranger.

The stranger was so angered that he left the print of his hand in the solid rock while playing his final card. And Kincheler realized at that point that he had been playing cards with the devil.

8

The Black Stag — In the year 1804 there lived at St. Bride's (then called Distress) a very respectable family named Conway. Thomas, the eldest son, was a strong man and a great hunter. One fine day he decided to visit his father who lived in Point Lance, several miles away. He harnessed his pony to the catarmaran which he loaded with produce for his father. He also brought along his gun and powder horn in case he saw some game along the way.

About halfway on the journey, Thomas suddenly saw a magnificent black stag in front of him. He quickly grabbed the gun and fired. To his surprise the bullet had no effect on the animal. He hastily retreated and fired once more. The stag still stood unmoved. In disgust Thomas carefully loaded the gun, this time with a double charge. He aimed carefully and fired. He was certain he had hit the stag. But to his amazement he discovered that the stag was still unharmed.

Thomas was alarmed and felt there was something uncanny about this beast. He jumped on the catamaran and quickly headed for Point Lance, where he told his father and friend about the stag incident. They laughed at him and said it was only poor markmanship. It was getting dark and Thomas decided to return home without delay.

About two hours later Thomas's wife became very alarmed when she saw his pony gallop into the yard alone. There was no trace of Thomas on the slide. A search began and Thomas was found in the exact place where he had reported seeing the stag. He was stretched out dead, with the contents of the powder horn scattered over his face. There were no marks of violence on him. What had killed him or what had frightened the horse? These are questions which have never been answered.

A short time after the incident Thomas' wife decided to go to Placentia to have her child christened. She was accompanied by his brother and a friend. On their return, at the same place where Thomas had died, something equally mysterious happened to them. They were all found dead. Their tracks indicated where they had met something that had itself left no trace. They had apparently run about in blind terror.

The mystery was never solved.

The Holyrood Ghost — A priest who didn't take seriously the threats of a dying man was haunted by the man's spirit at Holyrood. James Curran, who had settled at Holyrood from County Wicklow in Ireland, did not want to be buried in the graveyard on the north side of the community: the graves there were filled with water. He demanded that after his death he was to be buried in the graveyard on the south side of the community.

Curran's last words were that his spirit would haunt those responsible if his dying wish was ignored. When family and friends of Curran protested the Church's plan to bury him on the north side, it became necessary for the parish priest to intervene.

The priest was Father Carm Walsh. He told the mourners, "We will bury this old Irishman in the north-side burial ground, and I will take him over myself and let him come back and haunt me." Against his dying wishes old Curran was buried in the north-side graveyard.

That night while returning home from visiting parishioners, a sudden snow-storm struck and Father Walsh became lost. He arrived home during the early morning hours and was greeted inside by the spirit of old Curran. Old-timers claim that Curran's spirit had led the priest astray. Whatever happened that night we can only speculate. However, the following Sunday the parish priest made arrangements to move Curran's body to the south-side graveyard, thereby fullfilling his dying wish. The new grave site was blessed by Father Walsh, and a special mass was celebrated in memory of James Curran.

The Banshee — This tragic tale involving the supernatural had its beginning during the Middle Ages in Ireland and concluded near the end of the 18th century in a home located on the Hill-o-Chips in downtown, St. John's.

Most families in St. John's at that period had some strange tradition or unusual token associated with them. The family of city businessman William Welsh was associated with the cry of the Banshee. Although Welsh dismissed the tradition as so much Irish foolishness, his wife and three sons did not.

Welsh, a healthy and robust fellow, operated a public house and banquet hall from his premises on the west side of the

Hill-o-Chips. His wife was widely known and respected as an excellent cook, and the banquet hall was famous for its affairs.

One night, Mrs. Welsh became terror stricken when she heard the cry of the Banshee at her window. By the time she alerted her husband it had disappeared. Describing the Banshee cry, Mrs. Welsh told her husband, "It was like a weirdly wailing and sobbing Keyne, coming nearer and nearer each moment until it reached the window. Then with a wild shriek it died away with unearthly sobbing. Anyone hearing it would never forget it."

The next day the Welsh's youngest son Felix cut an artery while cutting fire wood and came close to death. Still, William would not acknowledge belief in the Banshee.

Some years passed and on the occasion of his 60th birthday he found himself sitting at the head table in his banquet hall. He was accompanied by the most prominent citizens of St. John's, who had come to celebrate Welsh's birthday.

Suddenly the door swung open. Framed in the doorway, with a deathly pale face, stood William's eldest son Michael. He was oblivious to all else except his father — at whom he stared. A sudden silence fell as he made his way towards his father. "We all heard the cry tonight," he said. "Are you all right." William, somewhat surprised, answered, "Of course I am. Why wouldn't I be? I'm as healthy as an ox."

When Michael left the room, Colonel Skinner of the regiment in St. John's asked William what Michael meant when he referred to . . . "The Cry." William then told the attentive audience the story of the Banshee. He said that, "The Welsh's since time immemorial were from the Chiefs of a Baroney in Ireland, and from the first Welsh, a great Chief and Warrior, the Banshee's cry always foretold either a death or some ill fortune of one of them."

He added that although it was only tradition his wife and sons firmly believed in it. When he concluded his story many in the room agreed with the family. Colonel Skinner, however, was a little doubtful. But he expressed the opinion it was certainly a colorful piece of folklore.

When the guests left, Welsh scolded his wife and children for allowing a silly superstition to bother them. He said, "No one should concern himself about me; I never felt better in my life." The family then retired for the night.

11

The following morning at breakfast, without any warning or indication that something was wrong, Welsh died. When Colonel Skinner heard the news he was shocked. "I can't believe it." He was so healthy." he said. But then, recalling Welsh's tale of the Banshee, he added, "There was something in the Banshee's cry after all."

Chapter II
Strange and Unusual

There have been many strange and unexplained happenings throughout Newfoundland history. Intriguing and mysterious stories like the story of the mystery ship **Resolven** and the sighting of a mermaid in St. John's Harbour. There are some astounding stories, including the strange happening at the Roman Catholic Church in Avondale and the unusual answer to a children's novena at Ferryland. Other stories in this chapter include the strangest coincidence to take place anywhere, a remarkable psychic experience of a Newfoundland seaman, and a miraculous answer to a father's prayer in St. John's.

The Mystery Ship — Among the great mysteries of Newfoundland history is the story surrounding the *Resolven*. The *Resolven* arrived at Harbour Grace in 1884 with a cargo of salt for John Munn and Company. From there she was scheduled to go to Labrador to take on a cargo of salt cod for destinations in Europe. On board were four Newfoundland passengers. They were Thomas and George Colford and Douglas Taylor from Carbonear, and Edward O'Keefe from Harbour Grace.

The *Resolven* set out from Harbour Grace on August 27, 1884. A few days later the British gunboat *Mallard* sailed close by the *Resolven,* off the coast near Catalina. The *Resolven* was behaving erratically. The crew of the *Mallard* shouted as they neared the ship but they got no response. There was only the sound of waves beating against both ships.

The British sailors boarded the *Resolven*. The first thing they noticed was that the vessel's planking was scraped and rubbed above the waterline. There was also some minor damage to the sails. But after searching the vessel from top to bottom the British were completely baffled.

There was absolutely no sign of life anywhere on the mystery ship. They found clothing and other personal items of crewmembers throughout the ship left undisturbed. Adding to the mystery was the galley scene: there the table was set for a meal and the fire in the stove was still burning.

The *Mallard* then searched the area for any signs of crew and passengers, but found none. The *Resolven* was towed to Catalina, and the outside world became aware of the great mystery.

There was the suggestion that the Captain, crew and passengers had left ship in a hurry because it was approaching an iceberg. However, experienced seamen would have known that a boat can lie beside an iceberg for hours just the same as it would lie beside a ship. Most sea captains would have sheltered from the storm in this manner.

What happened to the *Resolven?* That's still a great mystery — more than 100 years after it occurred.

THE MERMAID — A strange story from our past is the one recorded by Sir Richard Whitbourne. He described coming face to face with a creature in St. John's Harbour that strongly resembled a mermaid.

The creature described by Whitbourne appeared again a few miles from St. John's Narrows during 1912. The two fishermen who witnessed the appearance described it as a mermaid. The men said they saw the creature come up from the ocean and try to climb aboard a dory near them. The dory belonged to two fishermen from Little Bay West.

The creature looked around, then came over to the boat and tried to climb into it. The fishermen fought it off and it disappeared into the ocean. The description of the creature of 1912 was similar to the one given by Whitbourne over 150 years before. He wrote in his diary, "The creature came to within the length of a long pike from me and was about 15 feet long. I was standing by the riverside in the Harbour at St. John's when it very swiftly came swimming toward me looking carefully at my face, like a woman. The face seemed to be beautiful and well proportioned. It had about the head many blue streaks resembling hair but it certainly was not hair.

St. John's Harbour, where Sir Richard Whitbourne claimed to have seen a Mermaid — photo, Jack Fitzgerald.

"It later came to the boat and put both hands on the side. This frightened the crew and one of them struck it hard on the head causing it to fall back into the water. The men in the boats were frightened by the creature and fled to land."

What was this strange creature? Some suggested it was a seal, but others noted that a master like Whitbourne and experienced Newfoundland fishermen would have known a seal if they saw one.

The creature was never accurately identified, but Sir Richard Whitbourne felt it was a mermaid.

A Strange Coincidence — Two vessels, storm-tossed on the North Atlantic, in incidents years apart but traveling identical routes, formed the basis for one of the strangest coincidences in all Newfoundland history.

This strange happening involved Peter MacPherson, founder of the MacPherson family in Newfoundland and great-grandfather of the famous Dr. Cluney MacPherson (inventor of the gas-mask).

Peter arrived in Newfoundland at the age of 17 in the year 1804. He founded the MacPherson business at Port de Grave in 1811. He later married the daughter of Joseph Furneaux and they had three daughters.

The strange coincidence took place when Peter was returning to Newfoundland accompanied by his aunt after vacationing in England. Their ship was approaching the harbour at St. John's; it was so close that Peter could actually see his home in downtown St. John's.

It was at this point that the strange story began. A sudden wind came up and blew the ship out to sea. The winds increased and caused damage to the ship's mast. When the storm subsided the crew rigged jury masts; but just as they finished, the storm resumed even more fiercely than before. It blew the ship clear across the Atlantic to the west coast of Ireland.

Meanwhile, people in St. John's who had witnessed the sudden storm and the disappearance of the ship had given up hope. They believed the ship was lost at sea with all hands on board.

While the people at St. John's discussed the tragedy, the passengers and crew were safe in Ireland waiting for the completion of repairs to their damaged vessel. To pass away the time Peter MacPherson visited some of the Irish cottages in the village. In one of these he saw a painting of a man who was strangely familiar to him. But he didn't know why.

The portrait impressed him so much that he asked his aunt to come and view it. She agreed, and when she saw the portrait she gasped and almost fainted. When she regained her composure she said, "Why, Peter, that's your father." Peter MacPherson was only eight years old when his father died.

When asked where it came from the portrait's owner replied, "Oh, that washed ashore on the beach packed in a bale of goods. We liked it and hung it up." Peter purchased it, and when the ship was ready for sailing he took it home to Newfoundland. The strange coincidence, however, did not end there. Peter learned that his father had the portrait painted in England and packed in a bale of goods to take with him to Newfoundland. His father's vessel set out and followed the same route that young Peter's vessel had taken years later. That vessel also ran into a storm, and sank off the coast of Ireland. There were no survivors. Debris from the wreck had washed ashore at the same place Peter's vessel put in at Ireland years later.

Two vessels, storm-tossed, on the same voyage, years apart, one lost, the other saved, one with the portrait of the father, the other carrying the son — the odds of them coming together were fantastic. Yet it did happen. The MacPherson portrait did not survive, however. It was destroyed in the fire that swept the city of St. John's in 1846.

A Truly Amazing Story — The people of Western Bay went into mourning after being told that Captain Jim Halfyard had fallen overboard and was lost at sea. In keeping with the custom of the time, window blinds in homes throughout the community were lowered and flags flew at half-mast. The entire community went into mourning.

Hardly anyone noticed the arrival in the harbour of the brigantine *William*. However, the lowering of a boat and several men boarding it to come ashore did attract attention. The people knew the *William* was from Brigus and that there was no one on it from Western Bay. They wondered why they were being visited?

When the lifeboat neared shore those who had gathered to greet its arrival were shocked. They believed they were seeing a ghost. Seated in the stern of the boat, hale and hearty, was Captain Jim Halfyard — the man everyone believed to be dead.

The Captain's explanation of his survival at sea certainly belongs in the believe it or not category. All the crew of the Halfyard vessel were brothers of the Captain. On the night the Captain disappeared a thunder and lightning storm raged, with the wind blowing a gale and causing high rolling seas.

A sudden lurch of the ship knocked Captain Jim, who was at the helm, overboard. By the time his brothers discovered he was missing, the vessel had travelled far past him; and although they returned and searched the stormy waters, they couldn't find him. They then returned to Western Bay to report the Captain's death.

Meanwhile, about four hours after the Captains had fallen into the water the *William* passed by. Halfyard, nearly exhausted and ready to give up, made faint efforts to cry for help. On the *William* a crewmember heard the cries and persuaded Captain Whalen to go back and search. The seas were rolling heavily and there was heavy rain. There was no sign of anyone in the water.

Before giving up the search, Captain Whalen leaned over the side and extended a boat hook into the area where the crewman indicated the cries for help had come. Whalen felt the hook catch something and he pulled it up out of the water. It was Captain Jim Halfyard who had lost consciousness. He was revived, and Captain Whalen made a special trip to deliver him to his home in Western Bay.

Commenting on his miraculous rescue, Halfyard said, "Providence sent this noble ship and her crew to rescue me. It was a miracle how they found me in the darkness and the storm."

Another strange concidence — Two men who were boyhood friends went their separate ways after leaving school. Both became sea captains. The paths of the two, however, crossed again many years later in a most unusual coincidence during a raging storm off the coast of Nova Scotia.

Captain Joe Emberley was skipper of the *Wally G.,* a 68-foot schooner. A native of English Harbour East, Fortune Bay, Emberley had only one arm. His boyhood friend was Captain Lee Handrigan from nearby Rencontre East.

On this remarkable trip, Captain Emberley took his 17-year-old nephew on what began as a routine cargo-trip from Halifax to the Magadalen Islands. To save time he took a short cut through the gut of Canso rather than around Cape Breton Island. A sudden storm erupted. It was so violent, it wrecked the ship and sent her on the rocks at White Point.

When the ship went down Captain Emberley jumped away from the vessel, landing in the middle of floating but dangerous wreckage. He reached a large piece of the deck and managed to climb onto it. Then he made attempt after attempt to rescue his nephew, who was near exhaustion and clinging to the stern of the ship.

Each time he neared the boy he shouted for him to let go and swim to the wreckage. But the frightened boy was too weak to make the effort. Emberley said, "It was a terrible feeling to see a shipmate and a blood relative drown before your eyes."

The piece of wreckage on which Emberley was hanging began drifting out to sea. In desperation the Captain made repeated attempts to attract the attention of two passing schooners, but without success. By 5 a.m. the following morning Captain Emberley was near exhaustion. He couldn't summon strength to call for help to a ship sailing nearby. However, the Captain of that schooner was standing on deck and noticed something bobbing around in the water. He ordered a life boat to be lowered and went himself to investigate. James Emberley was astounded to see the man coming to his rescue was Lee Handrigan, the boyhood friend he had not seen in years. It was a re-union both men never forgot.

The Rainbow — On March 25th, 1842 a phenomena occurred in the skies over St. John's which prompted one Newfoundland historian to record the event in a book.

The phenomena was a bow that was not a rainbow nor did it display the ordinary colours of a rainbow. Lord Bonnycastle, in his 'History of Newfoundland', recorded that he was a witness to the unusual appearance. He noted, "On the evening of Good Friday, March 25th, 1842, with the thermometer at 30 degrees farenheit and a North-east wind, a most unusual appearance was exhibited at sunset around 6:30 p.m. "The western sky over St. John's was in a blaze of roseatte and fire colored angry light after the sun dipped a blaze which reflected on the eastern or sea sky to a great extent; and just as the sun had disappeared behind the hill, a perfect bow appeared in the east. This bow did not have the usual rainbow colours. It was made up of a variation of the colour red, from fiery red to the Rosette.

Bonnycastle noted that the phenomena was a perfect arch, of the usual size and height of a rainbow at sunset. He added that the previous evening the eastern sky at sunset was beautifully colored with purple and red down to the horizon, while the western sky was not. The thermometer varied only two or three degrees above or below freezing all the time; yet both these appearances were succeeded only by light thaws.

19

The historian wrote that while snow covered the land and ice lay off shore there was neither snow nor rain during the two days of the unusual phenomena. Some people thought it was the end of the world. The unusual rainbow of 1842 has never been explained.

A Little Miracle on Signal Hill — An unexplained incident involving the noon-day gun at Signal Hill, St. John's took place during 1890. The diptheria epidemic that raged throughout the city that year had spread to Portugal Cove. Among its victims were Canon Smith, the parson there, and his four children.

Through the efforts of Judge D. W. Prowse and Dr. Fraser, the Smiths were taken to the hospital on Signal Hill (this hospital was destroyed in the fire of 1892). Three of the Smith children had died and nine-year-old Harold was suffering through his last days on earth.

Parson Smith wrote in his diary of little Harold's final day. He noted, "A strong breeze of wind was blowing on the day that Harold died. He was a bright lad, but his nerves were highly strung and he was easily excited. While at 10:30 a.m. I watched him as he was lying quietly in his bed, the wind slammed one of the doors of the hospital.

"The noise so affected little Harold that his face became for a few moments distorted by pain and turned quite purple. After some considerable time he became easier. Glancing at my watch, I saw it was only four minutes to 12 noon, and then I thought of the noon gun which was planted above the hospital, right on the hill back of it.

"The report from that gun I knew would soon thunder over the hospital shaking the whole building. I was in an agony of mind as to what would happen then to little Harold."

Canon Smith was haunted by an incident many years before in which a young girl, viewing the motionless body of her dying father, screamed so loud that he sat up in bed and lingered for nearly two hours in horrible agony before death came to relieve his suffering.

Smith continued with his account of his son's last day: "I was beside myself with fear of what I believed would soon be enacted in the room where my boy and I were. Then a voice spoke to my inmost soul: 'Ask, it said,' and ye shall receive.'

"I can't remember exactly what I said in the agony of prayer on that occasion, but I think it was something like this: O Lord, who did shut the mouth of lions, of thy pity muzzle that gun. I thought that the great God would give his angels charge to shield my little lad so that he would not be disturbed by the report of the gun." Parson Smith watched the time until 1:00 o'clock but the gun didn't fire. He said, "I knew that God had answered by prayer. At 1:30 little Henry slipped peacefully into eternity."

A Mr. Scott was in charge of the noon day gun at the time, and he couldn't explain why the gun did not fire that day. He said, "Three times I put a new primer into her and pulled the lanyard, but the old girl wouldn't speak. It was all no use. I feared to prime her again least some fire might be in the vent and fire the gun while I was in the act of priming it. The next day I tried her again and she answered at once to the first pull of the lanyard."

When Parson Smith recovered he told his congregation at Portugal Cove about God's little miracle on Signal Hill.

A Newfoundland Psychic — Captain Frank Ash of Trinity Bay had a psychic experience that led to the rescue of seven survivors of an ill-fated Arctic expedition.

In 1881 the U.S. Government commissioned Lt. Adolphus Greeley, a U.S. Cavalry Officer, to carry out observations in the Arctic. The project involved 25 men and was very well planned. They took along provisions for three years and 140 tons of coal. The *Proteus,* under the command of Captain Richard Pike, a Newfoundlander, took the expedition to the Arctic and waited with them until they completed building a wooden house.

The party ran into problems a year later when the Newfoundland sealing vessel the *Neptune,* which was carrying supplies to the expedition, was forced to turn back because of severe ice conditions. On June 29, 1883, Captain Pike took his ship to a place called Payer Harbour, which was closer to Greeley's Party than the *Neptune* had gotten. This effort also ended in failure.

Ice crushed the *Proteus,* causing it to break up and sink. Captain Pike managed to get three lifeboats off before the ship went down. Pike and his 21-man crew hauled and rowed their lifeboats 800 miles to Disko, Greenland.

Meanwhile back in the U.S., Arctic experts began expressing doubt that Greeley and his party would ever be found. The U.S. Government offered a $25,000 reward to anyone who could locate the Greeley expedition.

The Americans hired a Newfoundland sealing vessel, the *Bear*, at a cost of $100,000, to search for the Greeley party. The *Bear* was a new steam ship built in Scotland and designed especially for Arctic ice. In addition to the *Bear* the U.S. engaged two other Newfoundland sealing vessels, the *Thetis* and the *Alert*.

The three-ship fleet was manned by 102 hand-picked American sailors under the command of Winifield Sachley. Two Newfoundlanders, Frank Ash of Trinity and a Captain Norman, were taken along as ice pilots. It was Captain Ash whose psychic experience lead to Greeley's rescue.

Ash had a dream in which he saw a house erected by Greeley's party. Ash later recalled that the location was etched in his memory when he boarded the *Bear* the next morning to begin the search. He directed the search according to the directions in his dream.

The group was encouraged to continue following Ash's suggestions after they found Greeley's records. Continuing on with the search they found Greeley and six other survivors. One man had lost both hands and feet. A spoon was tied to heal the stump on his right arm. The bodies of those who died were exhumed from their frozen graves and returned to the U.S. for proper burial. The survivors spent two weeks in St. John's before going home to the United States.

During that first Arctic expedition Greeley had discovered new land, north of the Greenland ice-cap. Greeley died in 1935 at the age of 91.

The Novena — During October, 1926, the Roman Catholic children at Ferryland made a Novena, praying for something good to happen to the community. Ferryland in 1926 was experiencing a particularly hard time. On the final day of the Novena one child impatiently asked the sister at the convent why nothing had happened. The sister piously replied, "The day isn't over yet."

It was some time before the good sister was able to live

down these words. Before the day was over a near-tragedy occurred that surprisingly did benefit many people in the community. The event was the wreck of the *Torhamvan*. The vessel
was enroute to Montreal when it ran aground in dense fog on
a point on the north side of Ferryland. For some time the people of Ferryland could hear the horn blowing but were unable
to see the doomed ship as she tried to manouver between Goose
Island and the reefs which threatened to trap her.

At 5 p.m. the sound of wrenching metal was heard through
the fog. At one point, an empty life boat drifted in to the beach,
causing great concern to bystanders, who felt sure the crew
had been drowned. However, it turned out to be an empty
boat which had fallen away from the ship.

Statues from the wreck of the *Torhamvan* displayed outside the Roman Catholic Church
at Ferryland. (photo — Jack Fitzgerald).

Mike Kinsella, Billy Williams and John Will Costello went
out in a small boat and successfully rescued everyone from
the ship. There was no loss of life — no tragedy although the
government impounded the cargo, a good supply of paint,
soap, jam, lard and macaroni found its way into a good many
homes.

The beaches at Ferryland were literally white with macaroni

for weeks afterwards. All that remains of the ship at Ferryland today are its boilers rusting away on the beach and the bronze statues on display outside the Ferryland R.C. Church.

Lower Island Cove — Sabbath Breaking

During the early days of colonization, missionaries to Newfoundland had a difficult job persuading the inhabitants that they should observe the Sabbath day with rest and prayer. Sunday was like any other day of the week; people jigged for squid, caught and salted fish, and hunted seals.

Lizzie Locke of Lower Island Cove was one of a minority of people who felt the Sabbath should be observed. Lizzie was one of the first Newfoundlanders to make a stand against spreading fish on the Lord's Day. This sometimes lead to conflict with her husband, who felt that the spreading of fish on the Sabbath was not a violation of the third commandment.

Lizzie's belief was put to the test at a time when her husband was away, leaving her with the responsibility of salting the fish or allowing them to spoil. All the fishermen and their wives went to the wharves on a Sunday and began to work on their catches.

One of the men went to ask Lizzie if she was ill and she answered, "I am not unwell, thank God, and I have not spread my fish because it would be breaking the Sabbath." The friend reminded her that if she failed to spread the fish she would lose the entire catch. She told him that she would rather lose the fish than lose her soul.

She also refused an offer from neighbours to do the work for her. It was a hot day and Lizzie was concerned over the possible loss of her catch. She prayed for strength and grace, to fight the temptation to work and save her catch.

At the end of the day as the others returned to their homes, they scolded Lizzie for being a 'religious fool' by allowing her fish to go unattended.

The following morning, Lizzie went to the wharf expecting to find her entire catch of fish spoiled. The neighbours went also, expecting their catches to be in perfect condition. What they found was instrumental in turning the entire community to God and the observance of the Sabbath.

The men and women who had worked to save their fish were shocked to see that the entire catches had been spoiled by the powerful rays of the sun. On the other hand, Lizzie Locke's catch which had not been exposed to the sun was not damaged. From that day the Sabbath was strictly observed at Lower Island Cove.

You Can Take It With You — There's an old saying that 'you can't take it with you', meaning when you go to the grave you take nothing material with you. Yet, there may have been an exception to that at Avondale, Conception Bay, during 1911. The story of Father John Roe and the Roman Catholic church at Avondale is one that belongs in *Ripley's Believe It or Not!*

Originally Avondale was a missionary post attended to by the parish priest at Harbour Main, Father Jeremiah O'Donel. After the death of Father O'Donel, Father Roe took over the post and developed a great love for the then-growing community of Avondale.

The Avondale church today. The first Avondale church was destroyed by lightning. (photo — Jack Fitzgerald).

Father Roe took on the project already started by Father O'Donel, to complete a church at Avondale. With enough lumber cut and piled to finish the church, a dispute broke out among the parishoners of Harbour Main and Avondale. The parishoners of Harbour Main demanded that the wood at Avondale be used for the church at Harbour Main.

Angered by the dispute, Father Roe took a strong stand in favor of Avondale, stating publicly that, "Avondale will be my church dead or alive." Alive he got his wish: the Avondale church was completed. In death he may have also gotten his wish. On June 17, 1911, Father Roe died suddenly at Avondale. At the same hour of his death lightning flared from the heavens, striking and destroying the Avondale church.

From Tailor to Millionaire — Tom Meagher, a St. John's tailor during the 19th century, became a millionaire and shipowner in a rather unusual way. He made a fortune and became owner of several foreign-going cargo vessels because of the War of 1812.

During that period there was almost a daily sale of cargoes of the prizes brought into St. John's Harbour by British naval vessels. By accident Meagher stumbled onto a deal during one such auction which made him a millionaire.

On that day there was a sale of crockery ware; however, there was already an oversupply of crockery in St. John's. Meagher entered a deal with another Water Street merchant named William Thomas, to go halves on the cargo and store it until there was a market for it.

Just as the auctioneer was about to close down the bidding, a military officer named Captain Barnes, who was well-known throughout the City for his practical jokes (and a little under the weather), made a successful bid for the works.

He said he would throw away the crockery and use the empty crates as chicken coups. The Captain left, allowing Meagher to take possession of the crates. Meagher intended to split the contents with Thomas and deliver the crates to the Captain. However, when he opened them he discovered a valuable cargo of the rarest valuable silks he had ever seen. Apparently they were being smuggled into the United States when the ship carrying them was intercepted by the British.

Meagher decided to keep the treasure for himself. He hid the silks, shared the crockery with Thomas, and delivered the crates to Captain Barnes. Meanwhile, Captain Barnes had sobered and was being threatened with courtmartial by his commanding officer for taking part in a commercial enterprise.

Meagher came to his rescue by offering to bail him out by paying for the crates. That fall Meagher secretly took his valuable cargo to Ireland and sold it. When he returned to Newfoundland in the Spring, he brought with him a whole cargo of goods for general trade and seemed to have an unlimited supply. Meagher became a millionaire and got into the shipping business. When he retired he returned to settle in Ireland.

The Kemp Fortune — James Kemp of Poole, England, who operated a shipping business at Carbonear during the early 19th century, made millions of dollars from Napoleon's blockade of Spanish Ports in 1810. At that time Napoleon was trying to keep the crown of Spain on the head of his brother Joseph, and the British had its fleet blockading Spanish ports.

Marshall Suchet, one of Napoleon's French Generals, had taken control of Southern Spain and the English had implemented precautions to make sure that no supplies could get through to him. Operating out of Carbonear, Kemp knew that if he could break through the blockade he would get top dollar for food cargoes.

He decided to take the risk. Two of his vessels, loaded with cod fish, managed to break through the blockade. The French paid top prices for the cargo. After discharging the fish the Newfoundlanders took on a cargo of French wine, which they purchased very cheaply. The wine was sold in London at fabulous prices.

Instead of selling the cargo in bulk, Kemp retailed the wine by the bottle and the glass, and accumulated a rapid fortune from the venture. After making his fortune from the blockade busting, Kemp retired from the Newfoundland trade, purchased a mansion in Poole, and got himself elected to the British House of Commons. Before he died he became one of the biggest landowners in Poole.

The Day Lindberg Got Lost — Charles Lindberg made world history by becoming the first person to succeed in making a solo flight non-stop across the Atlantic. He accomplished this on May 20th, 1927, when he flew from New York to Paris in his mono-plane, *the Spirit of St. Louis*. On that historic flight

27

Lindberg flew in over the Southside Hills at St. John's and out through the Narrows as thousands of citizens watched in amazement. When he flew over Bay Bulls, people there dropped to their knees and prayed for him.

Seven years later a fascinating piece of trivia took place when Lindberg returned to Newfoundland. Lindberg was scheduled to land his plane at Bay Bulls Big Pond on his way to a special expedition for Pan American Airlines in the North Atlantic. He was assigned to carry out a detailed technical survey for Pan Am to plan a Northern Trans-Atlantic Air Route.

The visit to Newfoundland received a lot of media attention, and thousands made their way to Bay Bulls Big Pond to get a glimpse of the world-renowned Charles Lindberg. Lindberg, however, was unable to find Bay Bulls. Instead he set down his plane on Quidi Vidi Lake in St. John's. He told reporters that it was difficult to spot Bay Bulls among the large number of lakes so he went on to Quidi Vidi to seek directions. Subsequently, he managed to make it to Bay Bulls, but he was 45 minutes late.

Monument to Charles Lindberg at Bay Bull's Big Pond. (photo — Jack Fitzgerald).

The Lindbergs stayed overnight in St. John's as guests of Leonard C. Outerbridge, who represented Pan Am in Newfoundland, and then went on to Labrador. At Labrador they teamed up with Major Robert Logan on the *S.S. Jelling,* which carried the technical supplies and equipment for the expedition. At that time Pan Am was operating an air-mail service along 2,000 miles of Alaskan coastline and planning to expand world-wide.

Another piece of trivia concerning Lindberg was that he refused to accept money, gifts or huge contracts in recognition and appreciation of his trans-atlantic flight. He accepted only the $25,000 prize money for succeeding in the flight. He received nearly a half million dollars in gifts but returned it all to the many donors (where possible) and gave the remainder to charity.

An Aviation Fraud — On October 9, 1929, a small aeroplane set down at Lesters Field behind Cornwall Avenue in St. John's. The arrival attracted a great deal of media attention. It was a Berling low-wing single-seater monoplane, painted orange with a black trim, and was piloted by Urban F. Dietman.

Although Dietman refused to comment on the purpose of his visit, there was local speculation that he was planning to try to set a record for crossing the Atlantic. He had ferried his plane from Roosevelt Field in New York. It was pure coincidence that brought him onto the same field used by Alcock and Brown.

Local interest heightened when a New Brunswick newspaper reported that the flight was a venture to promote trade relations because it was the first U.S. aircraft to land in New Brunswick. The paper also speculated that the trip had a connection with the estate of Sir Francis Drake.

Dietman's grandfather was Joe Drake of Carlton County, N.B., where the pilot had visited before sitting down at Lester's Field. One local writer put forward the theory that the Carbonear family of Francis Drake were direct descendents of Sir Francis Drake and they had gone first to Boston to settle during the 19th century. Dietman had mentioned this Newfoundland connection while he was staying in St. John's.

Adding to the mystery, Dietman changed the name of his aircraft to *the Golden Hind.* Then, accompanied by the French Consul in St. John's, R. H. K. Cochius, he set out for Harbour Grace to seek more information about Drake's descendent's in Newfoundland.

Dietman gave no indication that he was planning a transatlantic flight; the public believed he was merely tracing his family tree. On October 22nd, without any warning and with excellent flying conditions, Dietman surprised everyone by taking off out over the Atlantic.

He left a letter with Mr. H. Archibald of Harbour Grace with orders not to open it until he was gone. In the letter he apologized for the lies he told, and said he was setting out for London with enough fuel for 25 hours flying time. He stated, "Drake did not bring me here nor to London, albeit I am a descendent. Sorry if I hurt anyone's feelings. Many thanks."

He was last seen flying over Cape St. Francis, then disappearing. He was never heard from again. A later investigation determined Dietman was actually planning a trans-atlantic attempt. The only person aware of the mission was his wife. He had kept it a secret so authorities wouldn't try to stop him. He had been warned by the plane's manufacturer that the craft was not suited for a trans-atlantic flight.

Civil-War Gun Boat — One of the best-known vessels in Newfoundland during the early part of this century was the steam tug *D. P. Ingraham*. Research on the *Ingraham* has revealed an interesting aspect of its background. The Newfoundland tug was used as a gun boat during the American Civil War.

The *Ingraham* was built in 1864 at Philadelphia, constructed of white oak with copper fastened throughout. Following the Civil War she was sold to a Nova Scotian company, and in 1888 was purchased as a tow boat by the Newfoundland Towing Company.

Her jobs in Newfoundland included acting as a bait-protection patrol boat and taking the Supreme Court on Circuit around the island. In addition, she participated in many rescue jobs and many a sailor owed his life to her.

The tug made her last trip on December 5th, 1921, under the command of Captain Charles Moore. The vessel had been assigned to tow the cargo vessel 'Jean and Mary' to Twillingate. The two left St. John's at 4:00 p.m. on December 4th and the weather was favourable. The next day as they neared

Cat Harbour Island, the weather changed and it began snowing.

Captain Moore ordered a double shift at the stokehold and made an increased effort to reach Hamilton Sound before dark.

By 6:00 p.m. there were hurricane-force winds, which made movement above deck impossible. The heavy tow of the *Jean and Mary* was dragging the *Ingraham* astern. A few hours later Captain Moore felt certain they would soon smash upon the coastal rocks. To give the *Jean and Mary* a fighting chance Moore disconnected the tow line.

The *Ingraham* went ashore at a place called Fishing Rock. The crew began firing guns to signal for help. The lightkeeper in the area heard the guns and led a rescue party, which succeeded in rescuing all those on board. All that was found of the *Jean and Mary* was some wreckage in a small cove. No bodies were ever found.

Royal Blood — There are Newfoundlanders today who have Royal blood but will never be able to lay claim to any throne. These are the descendents of King William IV of England. When the King was a Prince, at the age of 22 and still a bachelor, he came to Newfoundland serving as Captain of the *HMS Pegasus*. The Prince had affairs with many local women, several of whom bore illegitimate children.

He did not ignore his illegitimate offspring in Newfoundland. As each came of age he arranged for their acceptance into the Royal Navy, with each one becoming an officer. King William was an uncle of Queen Victoria.

Chapter III
Newfoundland Connections

*From the refloating of the **Maine** at Havana to the con-
cealing of guns destined for the Irish Rebels, Newfoundland
has had its share of involvement in stories of international interest. In addition, Newfoundland has some interesting connections with figures and events made famous in world history.*

Guns for Irish Rebels — St. John's played a more intriguing role in the Irish opposition to British rule than most people realize. For example, on one occasion Irish rebel forces
concealed 50,000 rifles in a field in St. John's.

During the mid-nineteenth century, the Irish rebel movement known as the Fenian Organization had agents assisting
them in Newfoundland. Fenian supporters in St. John's helped
to smuggle 50,000 rifles, which had been purchased at Port-
land, Maine, destined for Ireland. The entire operation was
a top-secret one. The St. John's agents unloaded the guns from
a ship in St. John's Harbour and buried them in a field located near the home of the Anglican Bishop of Newfoundland.

When a ship had been engaged to carry the weapons to
Ireland, the agents removed them from their hiding place and
loaded them on board. The cargo safely reached Kinsale,
Ireland, its destination.

The field in St. John's where the Fenians hid the guns was
an area once owned by Sir E. M. Archibald, one-time Attor-
ney General of Newfoundland. It was known as Bishop's
Thorpe (later Bishop's Court).

Remember The Maine — "Remember *The Maine!*" was the battle cry that inspired the American military during the Spanish-American War. It was the sinking of the U.S.S. *Maine* in Havana Harbour on February 16, 1898, that sparked the Spanish-American War. For several years after the war ended, the Americans held memorial services directly over the wreck of the *Maine* and laid wreaths on the masts projecting out of the water, in memory of those who died in the sinking and whose bodies were still entombed in the wreck. The sunken *Maine* had become an unofficial National War Memorial.

But in 1905 a salvage company sought to turn the *Maine* into a commercial venture. The company planned to construct a cofferdam around the *Maine,* drain the water from it and open it to visitors for a fee. The *Maine* was valued at five million dollars, and the salvage company got rights to it from the Cuban Government for a fee of five thousand dollars. If the effort failed the company planned to use the metals of the ship to make souvenirs and sell to tourists.

Captain John King of Arlington, New Jersey, was outraged at these plans. A veteran of the Civil War, having served with the Union Army in the three-day battle of Gettysberg, King was also a Newfoundlander.

King was born at Barnes Road in St. John's in 1841. At first he seemed to be the lone opponent of the commercial plans to exploit the *Maine,* but he was not deterred.

Captain King had a much earlier connection with the *Maine.* He had become a close friend of T. Estrada Palma while Palma lived in Arlington. When Palma returned to Cuba and became President, Captain King influenced his friend to bring about Cuban co-operation with the Americans in holding memorial services for the Maine victims in Havana Harbour.

King's letter-writing campaign to American newspapers lasted six years and the movement grew to include prominent military men and Congressmen. He persuaded the state of Maine to forward a resolution to Congress asking that the hulk of the *Maine* be removed from Havana Harbour and a decent burial given for the 63 men still on board. Newspapers began demanding it be refloated, mainly to determine what really caused its sinking. On March 10, 1910, Congress passed the bill to raise the *Maine* and notified King by special letter. The Maine was raised in 1911 and taken out to sea, where it was sunk in deep water.

Franklyn Expedition — During the mid-nineteenth century, Sir John Franklyn captured world attention by leading the famous Franklyn Arctic Expedition. His two vessels, the *Erubus* and the *Terror,* along with 129 officers and crew, were lost in the Arctic. For decades after they were themselves the objective of many search expeditions.

Franklyn's famous expedition had several Newfoundland connections. Sir John Franklyn had gained some valuable sea experience in North Atlantic waters as commander of the *HMS Trent,* which was owned by Captain David Buchan, who himself has a prominent place in Newfoundland history. The first Lt. on the *Erubus* was Henry Thomas Dundas Le Vesconte, a medical doctor from the Channel Islands who lived and practiced at King's Cove. Le Vesconte was a boyhood friend of world-famous novelist Charles Dickens. (Aiden Maloney, former Minister of Fisheries in the Smallwood administration, is a descendent of Le Vesconte).

The famous expedition got caught in two very severe winter storms. The blizzard made it impossible to break out of the ice and the ships were crushed, causing all on board to perish. While the expedition ended in disaster, it succeeded in establishing the existence of the North West passage.

Henry Le Vesconte first came to Newfoundland with Franklin. He married Amelia Whelan, the daughter of the lighthouse keeper at Bonavista, and settled at King's Cove. He had been chosen by Franklyn because of the knowledge he gained of the Berring Strait while serving with the Royal Navy.

When he departed for the expedition his mother gave him a Bible inscribed with the date of the departure. It was the discovery of this Bible, found by searchers in the snow, that enabled authorities to identify some of the skeletons found it as being from the Franklyn expedition.

The name Le Vesconte was prominent at King's Cove for many years. The homestead there was called Trafalga House.

President Roosevelt — During 1939, while Adolph Hitler was demanding that Poland give up Danzig or face partition, and the British were preparing for war, President Franklyn Delano Roosevelt of the United States was fishing on the Humber River in Western Newfoundland.

On August 18, 1939, the President arrived at Humber River

to begin a two-day fishing trip. He was travelling on board the U.S. cruiser *Tuscaloos,* escorted by the destroyer Essert.

The President's ship anchored at Petipas Cove at Summerside, which is opposite Corner Brook. That was the furthest north Roosevelt had been since becoming President. Records indicate the President had a successful and enjoyable trip and enjoyed fresh-cooked Newfoundland fish before returning to Washington.

Halley's Comet — Edmund Halley, famous in world history for discovering the comet which bears his name, once visited Newfoundland but was given a less than enthusiastic welcome.

When Halley sailed into St. Mary's Bay on July 31, 1676 aboard the *Paramour,* a heavy fog blanketed the area and the *Paramour* became lost. Some French fishermen came to the rescue and guided the *Paramour* to safety.

When the fog cleared, the ship continued along the Newfoundland coastline; but when they came within sight of some Newfoundland fishermen, the Newfoundlanders fired at it. Halley's ship gave chase and when they caught the Newfoundlanders they learned that the fishermen had thought the *Paramour* was a pirate ship. Halley accepted the explanation and pardoned the Newfoundlanders for their attack. The *Paramour* then sailed into Tors Cove and took on fresh water and birch wood. Halley was actually sailing to Boston from Bermuda when a heavy storm forced him to change course and head for Newfoundland.

Halley had been commissioned by the King to sail the Atlantic to gather knowledge of longitude and variations of the compass. Of special concern was the problem of finding longitude at sea. Halley felt it could be determined by using a magnetic variation, but his idea never worked.

Edmund Halley's place in world history was earned when he successfully predicted that the comet sighted in 1862 would return to earth every 75 years or so. That comet, which was first sighted around 240 B.C., was named Halley's Comet. Halley, England's Second Astronomer Royal, headed the famous Greenwich Observatory for 22 years.

Castro's Hostage — During June, 1958, when Fidel Castro was leading his rebels in their battle to oust President Batista, his army burst into a cafe and took several hostages. The hostage-taking captured newspaper headlines around the world.

Among those captured was Ed Cannon. Cannon had arrived in Cuba just a few months earlier on a project for Steadman Engineering, on contract with Bowater's Ltd. of Corner Brook. He had left Corner Brook for Cuba during March to work on the Moa Bay Nickel Mining Operation. He was one of two Canadians in the group taken hostage.

It was June 26, during an evening of relaxation outside the company town, when Castro's rebels burst into the Cafe from all entrances, armed with machine guns.

Cannon recalled, "We were placed in trucks and then driven into the hills for about 40 miles to the rebel's centre of operation, which was a large house with no furniture on a coffee plantation. There we lived like millionaires for a week or two until negotiatiors secured our freedom. We were flown out by helicopter, two at a time to Guantanama Air Base and then to the U.S."

He said the hostages were treated well by the rebels. He noted, "We were given cigarettes, food and an occasional beer, of which the rebels deprived themselves. We had some anxious moments. On one occasion we were herded into a room and could see guards obviously angry in a nearby room preparing their guns for action." Cannon explained that he learned later that this was in response to Batista's planes flying overhead.

Cannon also recalled that they were never ill-treated or intimidated by their captors. Both Fidel and his brother Raoul were at the camp and in good spirits. He noted, "When we were leaving Castro gave me an arm patch of the rebels and autographed it. I gave him a company ball-point pen.

After being released, Cannon returned to his job at Corner Brook.

Rags To Riches — A young man, who narrowly escaped death during a shipwreck at Cape Race, left Newfoundland penniless and went on to become one of the richest and most powerful men in the state of New York.

On June 30th, 1840, 14-year-old Michael Adrian, accompanied by his mother and younger brother, boarded the passenger vessel *Florence* at Rotterdam. They hoped it would take them to the New World and a new life. The *Florence* carried an eight-man crew under the command of Captain Sam Rose, in addition to 79 passengers.

The trip was pleasant until August 19, when a thick fog engulfed the vessel off the coast of Newfoundland. The winds intensified and the **Florence** was crushed upon the rocks at Cape Race. She began filling with water, and many of the passengers gathered their gold and silver before attempting to swim to shore. However, the weight of the gold and silver dragged them to the bottom.

Meanwhile, the Captain and crew risked their lives by swimming ashore with a rope which they used to bring the survivors ashore. During this rescue attempt young Adrian took his mother on his back and helped her safely to shore. Thirty of the 79 passengers made it to safety with no belongings except the clothes on their backs.

They journeyed through thick bogs and woods, and over bleak and rugged hills, in search of some human habitation. Surviving on only berries and water they reached the community of Renews. There they were taken into the homes of the people and given food and warm clothing. Later they were taken to St. John's, where the public donated food and money to assist them in getting to New York.

The Adrians arrived in New York penniless, having lost all their belongings and wealth at Cape Race. Michael, however, accomplished great things. He became the largest landowner in New York, founded the German Exchange Bank, and later took over the First National City Bank of New York.

Chapter IV
Fascinating People

The Newfoundland influence has spread throughout the world. Our history records a litany of the names of those New-foundlanders who travelled all over the world and accumu-lated great wealth and fame for their deeds. In my search for the unusual and odd from Newfoundland's past, there seems to be an endless list of intriguing, fascinating and famous New-foundlanders (or people of renown with connections with New-foundland). This chapter continues this list of fascinating people where my two previous books on this subject left off. I am referring of course to 'Jack Fitzgerald's Notebook' and 'Amazing Newfoundland Stories.'

Patricia Murphy — During the 1970's Patricia (Murphy) Kiernan would often pilot her own private aircraft from New York to Florida, spend a few days resting at her 48-acre luxu-ry estate there and then return to New York to operate her multi-million dollar restaurant-chain business.

Mrs. Kiernan was a successful New York business-lady who had received the rare Papal Honor of Lady of the Equestrian Order of the Holy Sepulchre of Jerusalem. Her story is of in-terest to Newfoundlanders because Mrs. Kiernan was the form-er Patricia Murphy of Placentia Bay.

She first arrived in New York during the fall of 1929 with a scholarship to study music. She had been born during the early 1900's, the daughter of Frank Murphy, a general-store operator at Placentia. Shortly after arriving in New York, while living with her uncle, she decided to drop her musical studies and strike out on her own. She rented a furnished room in Manhatten for four dollars per week, and got several part-time jobs. These included playing the piano during lunch hours at a restaurant near Columbia University, working in a cafeteria, and hand coloring postcards at three dollars per hundred.

One day in 1929, at the start of the depression, she dropped in for her usual 45-cent lunch at the Step-In Restaurant in Manhatten. But the restaurant had gone out of business. She decided to operate the business herself, and made arrangements to rent the place for $25 per week. She changed the name to the Candlelight and introduced her own speciality, called popovers. In 1938 she purchased a second restaurant in Manhatten and later another at Long Island. Eventually she had a chain of ten luxurious Candlelight restaurants, with her main one catering to one million customers a year. She also owned several gift-shops in Florida.

At one of her restaurants she had an 800-car parking-lot, with a special limousine shuttling-service to take customers to the main entrance. It included a pond, a bridge and a dazzling assortment of flowers and plants.

She married a New York stock broker in 1930 but that marriage was annulled. In 1948 she met Navy Captain James E. Kiernan at a New Years Eve party. They were married shortly afterwards, but Kiernan died in 1954.

Patricia owned a spectacular estate in Florida, which included greenhouses, a swimming pool, a marble cabana, and 48 acres of floral beauty, illuminated at night by thousands of lights.

She had a special interest in horticulture, specializing in orchids. She extracted perfume from them and marketed the perfume under the names of Green Orchid, Gold Orchid and Regina Rose.

Patricia Murphy won recognition in this field, and for her outstanding flowers won numerous awards, including a commendation from Queen Wilhelmina of the Netherlands.

The French Emperess Eugenie's Newfoundland Connection — William Johnston, one of the founders of the prominent Newfoundland firm Baine-Johnston, was a cousin of the wife of Napoleon III, the Emperess Euguenie of France, and even made a strong effort to visit her in Paris. Aides to

Napoleon blocked Johnson's attempt because they suspected he was a conspirator against the Emperor.

The incident began while Johnston, researching his family tree, discovered a connection with the family of the Emperess and another famous figure in history — El Cid Campeador of Spain. Johnston's search established a relationship between his family and the Earl of Fingal, who held the position of British Ambassador to the Spanish court at Madrid, one of the highest honors given by the Crown at that time.

The Earl's daughter married a Spanish Don who was a descendent of El Cid Campeador. This daughter was an ancestress of Empress Eugenie. While the branch of the family bearing the Earl's name had died out, the family fortune remained unclaimed in London. Johnston gathered his evidence and set out for Paris to meet with the Empress, to establish the link that would assure both of them a claim to the fortune. Johnston had no difficulty with his business connections, in persuading some very influential people to give him letters of introduction to the French Court. For a week he was treated well and entertained by members of the French Court, who were impressed by his claim to be a relative of the Empress. But Johnston spoke very little French; and by the end of the week French officials became suspicious — during this period Napoleon had to contend with powerful enemies in his own country.

One newspaper editor so strongly believed Johnston was a conspirator that he refused to help him in any way. Based on these suspicions, Napoleon's aides refused to allow him to see the Empress. Johnston returned to Newfoundland in disgust; but after recovering from his disappointment, he delighted in telling his friends what an insurmountable difficulty it is, at certain times, to have a friendly chat even with one's cousins.

Rockwell Kent — A world-famous artist and one-time winner of the Lenin Peace Prize once lived in Newfoundland, but was ordered to leave by the Government because of suspicions he was a German-spy.

Rockwell Kent chose Newfoundland to settle in and bring up his family because of the picturesque difference between it and most other parts of North America and the much different pace of living. He rented a Victorian style house at Brigus. After repairing it and bringing it up to living standard, he sent for his wife and three daughters in the United States. Although the local people were indifferent about Kent's work as a painter, the Kent family was quickly welcomed into the community.

While World War I was raging in Europe, people in the Brigus area were becoming suspicious of Kent. The first rumor to spread was that he was a German spy and was actually painting maps in the studio he kept under lock and key. Noticing a large tool chest at the Kent homestead, some folks expressed the belief it contained a bomb or the tools to make one.

When Kent stored seven tons of coal for the coming winter an added spy suspicion was born. This time people said he was storing the coal as fuel for German U-boats operating in the Atlantic. If anything further was needed to prove Rockwell Kent was a spy, it was his singing German songs at a school concert.

Kent was aware of what his neighbours were saying and he found it all quite amusing. He posted a sign on his studio which read 'Chart Room', another room was called the 'Wireless Station', and his work shed was a 'Bomb Shop'. Under each sign he painted a German Eagle.

If Kent wasn't taking the accusation serious the Government in St. John's was. A CID officer was sent to question him. He confronted him by saying, "You look like a German." When Kent ignored the comment, the CID officer asked, 'Did you ever see one.' Again the police officer was treated with stony silence. He told Kent that he must visit the Inspector General in St. John's. It was a stormy session. Weeks later he was ordered out of Newfoundland. When told by a police constable to leave, he surprised him by saying simply, "Well, I guess, I'll go." The police sent an officer to the departing ship to make sure the Kents were all on board.

When Joey Smallwood learned of this injustice in 1967, he invited Kent and his wife to Newfoundland for a visit. A banquet was held in Kent's honour during July, 1968. When Kent saw the great changes in Newfoundland he said to Smallwood, "Why not let us have you on lend-lease for awhile? My God, how we and all mankind need men like you today."

The Cod Trap Inventor — The invention of the cod trap, which had such widespread affects on the fisheries of the world, came about almost by accident. The inventor was William Henry Whitely, a member of the Newfoundland Legislature, a man who lived thirty years on the coast of Labrador in a little settlement called Bonne Esperance.

Whitely was an American by birth and a Newfoundlander by choice. He was born at Boston on June 5, 1834. At the age of 13 he took a job as a printer. In 1851 he stowed away on the schooner bound for Labrador, which took him to Bonne Esperance. There he was taken in by an Englishman, with whom he lived for eight years.

In 1859 he went to England to settle an estate he inherited. In London he met and married Louise A. Thompson. They settled at Labrador and had 12 children. At Bonne Esperance Whitely was the top man, and everyone called him the Boss. He was the post-master, magistrate and harbour master, and in addition he operated a business of his own. He was known to be well-read, intelligent, and a pleasing companion.

Whitely developed the idea for a cod-trap while fishing himself, trying to figure out what to do with the fish in an overloaded cod sein. Over the next three years he worked to improve the cod sein, an effort that resulted in his invention of the cod-trap.

He gave the cod-trap model to Captain James Joy of Job Brothers. Joy passed it on to Rope-walk at St. John's. There the first cod-trap was manufactured for a man named Snow at Quidi Vidi. Snow's first year using Whitely's invention was a failure, but the second proved to be a big success.

As use of the cod-trap spread some fishermen on the Labrador coast complained that the new contraption would deplete the salmon stock. A patrol boat was sent to the area and fishermen were ordered to remove the cod-trap from the waters. Whitely protested and campaigned for several years to persuade authorities to allow the use of his invention. The Whitely cod-trap is now used by fishermen of all nations.

Whitely was elected to the Newfoundland Legislature in 1889, but declined to seek re-election in 1901. He passed away in 1903.

George Washington's Adversary — When George Washington led his American troops in his successful struggle for independence, one of his main adversaries was a military leader born in St. John's. Henry George Clinton, born in 1735, was the son of Newfoundland Governor Henry Clinton. Young Clinton was a brilliant young man who enlisted with the British forces while still a teenager. His intelligence and courage sent him rapidly up the ladder of military promotion. During the Seven Years War he distinguished himself under the command of Ferdinand of Brunswick. He was later elected to the British Parliament and knighted by the King of England.

During the American War of Independence he was initially second in command of British Forces in North America under Sir William Howe, and following the British defeat at Bunker Hill took full command. In this capacity he matched military skills with the great George Washington. It was Clinton, a Newfoundlander, who captured the City of New York and held it for most of the war. Following the British defeat by Washington, Clinton became Governor of Gibralter, where he died in 1795.

He had two sons who also became Generals. His son Henry fought in the Battle of Waterloo.

Other famous Newfoundland-born military men included General Sir Henry Pynn, who was born at Bristol's Hope and served as one of Wellington's generals; General Sir John Shea, who was in command of British Forces in India from 1928 to 1932; and George Bride, who was an Admiral in the British Navy. He was also author of several distinguished books on the art of naval warfare.

Famous Broadcaster — One of the top names in American broadcasting during the first half of this century was radio and television broadcaster Frank Knight. Knight was best known as the announcer for the Columbia Broadcasting System's television program, "Chronoscope", sponsored by the Longine Watch Company. He also hosted the Longine Symphonette, a popular weekly classical musical broadcast throughout both the U.S. and Canada.

Historians say, "Knight had the kind of voice that bordered on the pompous but was very popular." In 1952, Jack Gould, the television editor of the *New York Times* wrote that Mr.

Knight's commercials were delivered with, "an almost cathedral formality. They tend to induce such a feeling of social inadequacy that a viewer might be forgiven if he found himself wondering whether he was really eligible to buy the product."

Knight was born at St. John's; and following service with the Royal Newfoundland Regiment during World War I, went to McGill University intending to study medicine. But he gave it up after a year for an acting career. He had parts in several Broadway shows, including 'House Unguarded', but found that his voice could be used to better advantage in radio. In 1926 he began as an announcer with WABC in New York. One of his assignments was covering the arrival of the German Graf Zeppelin in 1928. The following year he joined CBS.

Knight became a household name throughout the United States. He passed away at a New York hospital on October 18, 1973; succumbing to burns sustained in a fire that swept his apartment a week earlier. His wife, Mildred Wall, also of St. John's and a one-time Broadway actress, also died in that fire. Knight was 79 years old when he died.

Benedict Arnold — In the United States, the name Benedict Arnold is synonymous with the word traitor. Arnold once visited St. John's, and developed a friendship with George Cartwright of Labrador fame. Arnold joined the American armed forces after the outbreak of the American Revolution. As an officer, he led attacks on several British forts. His outstanding leadership earned him a rapid advancement to the rank of general. On October 7, 1777, he led American forces in a successful battle against the British at Bemis Heights.

After that success he defected to the British and became an officer in the British forces. In 1780 he led his British troops in an attack which destroyed Richmond, Virginia.

When the war ended Benedict Arnold set up a small business in New Brunswick. In 1786 he set out for England to bring his family to New Brunswick. He travelled to St. John's to arrange passage to England. He and Cartwright became friends and shared a cabin on the brig *John of Teignmouth*, England.

Arnold and Cartwright brought along some supplies for their own use. These included two sheep, several hens, a good supply of vegetables, and other provisions. During the trip a sudden storm struck and the sheep were washed overboard.

45

Most of the provisions were lost as well.

To cope with this emergency the crew and passengers were placed on strict rationing. Arnold's traitorous character surfaced during the emergency when he secretly swaped a supply of wine belonging to himself and Cartwright for a supply of water from the crew's rations. He hid the water for his personal use, and Cartwright only learned of his friend's deceit when they arrived in England.

Famous Writer — The first English-speaking women in the world to be allowed to write about the Egyptian Royal Family and the Royal Palaces was a Newfoundlander from St. John's. She wrote travel books on Egypt, Lebannon and Jordan. She also wrote a book published in England entitled "Shepard's Hotel", the name of a world-famous hotel in Cairo. She was born in St. John's in 1915, and used the pen-name Nina Nelson. She was the daughter of Claude and Florence Noonan of St. John's.

Hugh Anderson — The story of John Murray Anderson, the famous Broadway movie producer who was born in St. John's is told in my book *Jack Fitzgerald's Notebook*. Not so well known is the story of his brother, Hugh A. Anderson, who also climbed the success ladder to fame and fortune in the United States.

Hugh Anderson teamed up with his famous brother in 1921 in the theatrical and motion-picture business. He became general manager and associate producer. During his association with his famous brother, they together produced 29 successful Broadway musicals.

From 1926 to 1929 Hugh Anderson directed a theatre school in New York; and among the many subsequent stars who studied under him were Bette Davis, Joan Blondell and Katherine Hepburn. He also wrote a book about his talented brother John, who passed away in 1954. That book was entitled, *"Out Without My Rubbers."*

Hugh was born in St. John's in 1890 and educated at Bishop Feild College in that city, Edinburg Academy in Scotland, and also schools in Switzerland and Paris. He served with the Royal Newfoundland Regiment in World War I and was decorated with the Military Order of the British Empire by King George V at Buckingham Palace in 1919.

Andrew Bulger — Andrew Bulger of St. John's earned a place in American history by capturing the Chief of the Sioux Indian tribe on the Mississippi and successfully bringing to justice a Sioux Indian wanted for murder. Bulger, who was only 25 years old at the time, was an outstanding military leader who displayed great endurance and courage in his role as Captain in the Newfoundland Regiment.

Bulger's story and the role of the Newfoundland Regiment in the American War of 1812 is not a well-known one but is worthy of preserving.

Major William McKay and Captain Bulger led an expedition of nearly 100 men of the Newfoundland Regiment, from Fort Mackinaw on the Great Lakes to the Mississippi River, 500 miles into American territory. The long trek was a challenging one for the Newfoundlanders. Bulger, in a letter to Colonel McDougal on December 30, 1814 stated, "Sir, I reached this place on November 30. From the moment of my departure from Green Bay, until my arrival here I experienced every misery in the power of cold and want to inflict. I suffered more, sir, during this voyage than you can imagine, much more than even I have suffered during the whole course of my life before. The morning we left to descend the Wisconsin River it was filled with floating ice and there was not a meal of victuals in any of the boats.

Despite the hardships, the Newfoundland force captured the Fort from the Americans at Praire Du Chien, and renamed it Fort McKay. Bulger returned to Canada that summer; but when the British learned that the Americans were planning to send an expedition to recapture the fort, they chose Bulger to return to command the fort against the attack.

When he arrived he found the Fort in a disorderly state. The Indians were acting up; there was a shortage of food; and some of the soldiers were insubordinate. Bulger quickly whipped the garrison into shape. When a Sioux Indian killed two British citizens, Bulger captured the Sioux Chief and held him as a hostage. He persuaded the chief to lead him to the murderer. When the chief came face to face with the murderer he told Bulger, "This is the dog that bit you." The Indian brave was tried, found guilty and shot by members of the Newfoundland Regiment. The Commander of the British Forces in North America, impressed with Bulger's leadership, confirmed his appointment as commanding Officer of Fort McKay.

Mike Shallow — A six-foot, 200 pound man from Newfoundland's Southern Shore gained international fame and recognition as a heavyweight boxing champion of Great Britain. That man was Mike Shallow. He was born at Fermeuse in 1874, and at an early age moved to Boston where he took up boxing.

His reputation as a fighter spread, and when he later returned to Newfoundland a major fight was arranged at the Prince's Rink in St. John's. The fight took place on August 8, 1904, between Shallow and Charlie Farrell, an international heavyweight fighter who had fought such greats as Gentleman Jim Corbett and John L. Sullivan. The Southern Shore native thrilled local fans by knocking out Farrell in the second round.

Boxing enthusiasts in Newfoundland were confident that Shallow was heading for the top of his profession, and on August 23 the same year they staged a benefit at the Prince's Rink to raise money to send Shallow to England for a crack at the British championship. By October Shallow was in England, fighting out of the National Sporting Club of London. One month after arriving he knocked out the former British heavyweight, Ben Taylor, in eight rounds.

After several more successes he got his chance to fight for the British championship. That famous battle took place on December 15, 1904, in Wales against British champ Jack Scales. After 10 rounds the fight ended in a draw, and Shallow's name was being spoken in sporting circles around the world.

Three months later the two met again, but this time the Newfoundlander knocked out Scales in the eighth round, earning himself the title of heavyweight champion of the British Empire.

In 1906 Shallow married Annie Foley of Brigus and settled at Pilley's Island, Green Bay. He later moved to Grand Falls to work as a pipefitter and also became fire chief there.

Mike Shallow passed away on July 1st, 1948, at the age of 74. Since that time he has been inducted into the Newfoundland Sports Hall of Fame.

Herbert Bown — Herbert Bown, a native of Badger's Quay, Newfoundland, during the 1970's invented the Telidon. The Telidon is capable of turning your television screen into a giant information centre. Observers speculated that the invention will propel Canada into leadership in the field of Electronic Information Gathering. The invention is already being used in many countries throughout the world, including the U.S., France, Japan, Great Britain, Germany and Australia.

One of the first private organizations to use the Telidon was *Time* Magazine, which in 1981 used it in its extension to electronic publishing, which delivers information to American cable companies. Another firm capitalizing on the invention was the *Los Angeles Times.* Bown's invention enables the storage of information in giant memory banks, and info that can be reproduced in home television sets.

Britain and France tried to develop their own Telidon's but without success.

Sidney Cotton — Sidney Cotton figures prominently in the aviation history of Newfoundland. He also earned a place in world history for an invention of his which was widely used in World Wars I and II. During 1916 Cotton invented the layered Sidcot suit. Although the invention was a world-wide success Cotton refused to accept any payment for it. Even the famous German War Ace Baron Von Richtofen was wearing a Sidcot Suit when he was shot down.

Cotton was born in Australia and fought with the Royal Navy Air Services in World War I. He came to Newfoundland in 1920, seeking contracts from Newfoundland sealing companies to spot sealing herds from the air. Although he had no success with that endeavour, he succeeded in recording many firsts in Newfoundland aviation history. He was the first to use an aircraft to deliver mail to communities isolated by winter. He was first to use an aircraft to search out large areas of timber on the island, and was also the first to utilize aerial photography to make aerial maps.

A little-known aspect of Cotton's life was the fact that he worked undercover for British and French Intelligence before the outbreak of World War II. Posing as a private businessman, Cotton secretly equipped his plane with remote-controlled cameras on the wings an photographed suspected military establishments in Germany and the Middle East.

When war broke out he modified a number of Spitfires to enable them to fly at greater speeds and to take picture from high altitudes. While in Newfoundland Cotton's inventiveness was put to good use. He invented a cover to keep the aircraft engine warm in cold weather; he used catalytic lamps under the aircraft's engine to prevent engine freezing, and equipped the aircraft with special winter survival gear.

John Ford — John Ford is one Newfoundlander who survived a nuclear attack. Ford, who hailed from Port aux Basques, served with the Royal Air Force torpedo squadron during World War II. He was captured by the Japanese and imprisoned a mile from Nagasaki. John Ford was working in the Mitubishi Naval Base with 350 Canadian prisoners of war when the American Aircraft *Boxcar 29* dropped the Atomic Bomb on Nagasaki.

When the bomb exploded, he said he looked towards Nagasaki and saw "a mushroom cloud forming over the city." He said there were pieces of steel flying, pieces of wood and everything seemed to blacken out. "The heat from it was like a blast furnace. When I felt it, I hit the ground." Ford continued, "After the mushroom, the whole sky blackened and the sun was completely obliterated with the heavy mushroom cloud. It was as if the sun had fallen out of the sky, and for a few minutes, until the clouds broke apart, it was pitch dark."

There was widespread panic. Ford recalled that there were 5,000 Korean girls in the Nagasaki camp. When the bomb hit they ran screaming in all directions. When the smoke lifted there were thousands of fires all over the area. The Japanese military took the prisoners to an air-raid shelter near the dockyard. Ford said the prisoners had no idea what had happened until two weeks later. He added that they knew something significant had happened because the attitude of the Japanese had changed. On August 18 an American plane flew over. By then the Japanese had painted the letters P.O.W. on the roof of one of the camps. Still puzzled as to what was happening, the prisoners asked for news using blankets to spell out the word news.

The Americans responded by dropping some pamphlets telling them the Japanese had surrendered. A month later, Ford was still in Nagasaki helping to clean up. The dockyard wasn't damaged, but Nagasaki was destroyed, with over 70,000 casualties. On September 13th Ford set out from Japan to return home to Newfoundland. When hostilities ended, Ford returned to the old job he had held prior to the War with the Newfoundland Railway. He retired in 1976.

Nicholas Darby — Around 1785 a Russian soldier passed away in a small village near Moscow. Nothing unusual in that — except this Russian soldier was born in St. John's in 1720, and for a few years had played a prominent role in the Newfoundland fishery.

In 1765, with the backing of the Newfoundland Governor, Sir Hugh Palliser, Captain Nicholas Darby attempted to develop the Labrador fishery. He set up headquarters at Cape Charles, where he built lodgings, a work shop and a fishing stage. He found survival in winter on the Labrador coast almost impossible, and met further trouble from the Inuit. Darby didn't give up his venture, however, and in 1769 he was back in Labrador, again trying to build a fishing industry. This attempt ended with authorities confiscating his goods and equipment on the grounds that he was illegally employing Frenchmen. Darby left Newfoundland and ended up in Russia, where in 1782 he joined the Russian Army. A few years later he died.

An interesting aside of the Darby story is that his daughter Mary Darby Robinson, also born in St. John's, was mistress of the Prince Regent of England who later became King George IV of England. She was nicknamed Peridita for the role she had played in the Shakespear play 'A Winter's Tale.'

Clarence Gosse — Clarence Gosse, a native Newfoundlander who moved to Nova Scotia, became such an outstanding figure in that province that he was appointed Lieutenant Governor.

During June, 1944, the 29-year-old Gosse was serving as a medical doctor with the Royal Canadian Army Medical Corps on the beach at Normandy. There he treated the injured and mangled caught up in the hell of the D-Day landing.

Dr. Gosse was also with the first Canadian Army hospital unit to cross the Rhine during the invasion of Germany. Following the war Gosse established a reputation as one of Canada's foremost surgeons and headed the Department or Urology at Dalhousie University. In addition, he became an active and successful farmer, a successful politician, and Chairman of the Nova Scotia Council of Health. In 1973 he was appointed Lieutenant Governor of Nova Scotia by Prime Minister Pierre Elliot Trudeau.

Sir William McGregor — Sir William McGregor, who served a term as Governor of Newfoundland during the early part of this century, was a noted botanist, minerologist and astronomer.

McGregor travelled throughout the world, particularly the South Pacific, and gathered large stores of information for the scientific community. Although numerous attempts had been made to cross the island of west Guinea by way of the Stanley Ridge, McGregor was the first to succeed. An indication of the difficulties encountered by the expedition was that one mile a day was often a high rate of progress. It was due to McGregor's great strength and courage that he succeeded where so many others had failed.

During this historic trek, McGregor discovered several new kinds of the famous Bird of Paradise, together with many other unknown specimens of animal and vegetable life. From New Guinea, which he succeeded in pacifying and bringing to order, he was transferred to Lagos, west Africa, a colony even more dangerous. During his rule there the annual mortality rate amongst white officials was reduced enormously.

When he became Governor of Newfoundland he took an immediate interest in studying the history of the Newfoundland fishery. Newfoundland had previously suffered because of lack of information on the fishery at the Colonial office. Sir William set himself the task to remove this obstacle, so that imperial authories would have the most trustworthy information in future negotiations regarding the welfare of the colony.

McGregor has the distinction of being the only Newfoundland Governor to be awarded the Albert Medal (civilian equivalent for the Victoria Cross). He was also awarded the Gold Medal of the Royal Humane Society of Australia, for saving several lives at sea at great risk to himself.

Professor Whiz — During the 1920's a magician in New York City grabbed international headlines by having himself manacled and placed in a heavy canvas bag, which was sealed tightly and thrown into the Harlem River. The magician, Professor Whiz, successfully escaped his shackles and the sealed bag. The entire demonstration was filmed by the Holyrood newsreel companies and covered by major U.S. newspapers.

Professor Whiz was the stage-name of Gerald Fitzgibbon, who was born in St. John's. His father, a merchant named Thomas Fitzgibbon, operated a wholesale-retail grocery store on Water Street just west of Buchannan Street.

Professor Whiz was as poplar in the U.S. as the famous Houdini; he toured every state in the Union, performing to sold-out houses everywhere. Young Fitzgibbon was inspired to become a magician after attending a performance of a magician-hypnotist known as Professor Lawrence at the Casino Theatre in downtown St. John's. Fitzgibbon befriended the Professor, who taught him to perform magic and to hypnotize. He became so skilled at hypnotism that on one occasion he hypnotized a customer in his father's store, placing him like a board connecting two barrels. He then piled up sacks of oats on him. Customers of the store were amazed at Fitzgibbon's skill.

After graduating from St. Bonaventure's College, Fitzgibbon moved to New York.

In addition to his skills as a magician and hypnotist, he became a great public speaker and was in much demand throughout New York as an after-dinner speaker. He was also a great athlete, and represented the Irish-American Club in many long-distance running events. Gerald Fitzgibbon, professor Whiz, passed away at Pensauken, New Jersey on January 14, 1955 at the age of 73.

Captain Cook — The famous Captain Cook, known in world history as a great explorer and navigator, owed much of his success to one-time Governor of Newfoundland Sir Hugh Palliser. Cook became a close friend of Palliser when they were both in their early twenties and serving on the H.M.S. *Eagle*.

Palliser was captain and Cook served under him as an able-bodied seaman.

Cook made a major contribution to exploring and surveying Newfoundland, and had many interesting connections with this country. In 1762, he was sent with a force of military engineers to rebuild the English forest on Carbonear Island, which had been destroyed by the French.

Sir Thomas Graves, Governor of Newfoundland at the time, made the British Admiralty aware of Cook's work, which helped him achieve rapid advancement to the rank of Captain. When Cook's old friend Sir Hugh Palliser succeeded Grave's as Governor of Newfoundland, Cook had already been appointed King's Surveyor. For this he was paid 10 shillings a day and given the best nautical and surveying equipment available at the time.

Governor Palliser appointed Cook Marine Surveyor of the coast of Newfoundland, and gave him his own survey ship, the 68-ton *Granville*. Up to that time the maps of Newfoundland, based on Jacques Cartier's explorations, made the major error of assuming Newfoundland was made up of small islands. Cook surveyed the coastline for four years before the completion of the first accurate map of Newfoundland.

During August, 1764, while hunting game in Western Newfoundland, Cook raised his gun to shoot a buck; as he reached for his powder horn the gun exploded in his hand. A doctor from a nearby French man-a-war treated him and managed to save the hand. However, it was deformed for the rest of his life. The scar ran from the wrist bone to the web portion of the thumb.

From Newfoundland, Captain Cook went on to discover British Columbia. On February 14, 1779, while exploring the Hawaiian Islands, he and his men were attacked by natives of the Sandwich Islands. After becoming separated from the rest of his crew, Captain Cook was butchered by the natives. Identification of his body was possible only by the scar on his hand, caused by his accident in Newfoundland.

Bill Doherty — One of the nuclear scientists working on the development of the Polaris Nuclear Submarine, which is now so vital to the defence of the free world, was a Newfoundlander born at Badger. He is the son of a man immortalized in the famous Newfoundland ballad, *The Badger's Drive:*

'Billy Doherty he is the manager and He's a good man at his trade
and when he's around seeking drivers, he's like a train going downgrade.
But still he's a man that's kind hearted, on his word you can always depend
And there's never a man that works with him, but likes to go with him again."

Billy Doherty had been brought to Newfoundland from Maine, in 1907, at the request of Lord Northcliff, to head up installation of river dams for the Anglo-Newfoundland Development Company. By 1915 *The Badger's Drive*, written by John P. Devine, was being sung all over Newfoundland and spreading the fame of Billy Doherty.

While living in Newfoundland the Dohertys had a son whom they christened William. They continued to live in Newfoundland until Billy was eight years old; then they returned to settle at Maine. Two year's later they came back for a vacation at Badger.

Billy grew up in Maine to become a prominent nuclear scientist. He lived at Kitty, Maine and worked on the Polaris missile submarine project at Portsmouth Naval Base.

During Come Home Year, 1966, Billy with his wife and son and mother Mary, returned to Newfoundland and visited Badger and the many friends of his deceased father.

Tom McDonald, who had worked with Doherty's father, had bought and was living in the Doherty's old homestead at Badger. McDonald had preserved old Bill Doherty's famous pikepole and presented it to Billy during the visit. In turn Dr. Doherty donated it to the Newfoundland Museum. The famous scientist was impressed with the improvements he found throughout Newfoundland. He commented, "The advancement in roads, industry and general appearance has been fantastic and Newfoundland seems to have much in store for her." While here he landed a seven-pound salmon, and a 490 lb. tuna at Conception Bay.

Jack Bursey — During the years 1956-1957 the United States established an air-base in Antarctica. A Newfoundlander who went to the Antarctic with Admiral Byrd played a key role in the operation.

Jack Bursey, who was born on the Northeast coast of New-foundland in a place called St. Lunaire, became an American citizen, then joined the U.S. Navy and rose to the rank of Lt. Commander. The base project was dubbed Operation Deep Freeze by the Pentagon, a scientific assault on the glacial ramparts of Antartica. Commander Bursey was decorated by the U.S. Government for his part in the operation.

Recalling his life in Newfoundland Commander Bursey said, "I was raised as a cod fisherman on the bleak rugged shores of the Northeast coast of Newfoundland. I was trained to know the sea and learned how to take care of myself in rough weather or smooth. When the ice broke up we coasted along the shores in our schooner, and as a boy I helped my dad bring her into a snug harbour on many a stormy night. In the winter I drove the team of dogs, our only transportation. I was hardened by the cold and the blizzards that blew over the coast."

Bursey was actually sent to the U.S. by Sir Wilfred Grenfell to attend school. In 1927 he responded to a newspaper ad looking for suitable people to join an expedition to the Antartic. Bursey was chosen from 50,000 applicants because of his Newfoundland background. He spent two years with Admiral Byrd during the exploration of the Arctic. This led to his assignment with Operation Deep Freeze.

He was leader of the group responsible for recognaissance. This group had the most important role of the entire operation. They had to blaze a 600 mile trail into the frozen wastes of Marie Byrdland, for the tractor-train that would follow to construct the base. The purpose of the base was to record simultaneous world-wide phenomena such as weather, magnetism, gravity, etc.

Bursey's letter of recommendation was addressed to Lt. Commander Bursey, Officer in Charge, Little America V, Antarctica. It read, "From November 1st, 1955 to March, 1957 you were a member of the wintering group that successfully constructed from the ground up, Little America V, Antarctica. During this period your competence, integrity, moral courage, ruggedness and untiring efforts contributed materially to the success of Operation Deep Freeze."

The Great Gallishaw — John Gallishaw was born in St. John's during the year 1890. After immigrating to the U.S. with his family and earning a degree from Harvard University, he went on to become a powerful and influential figure in Holywood.

In a career that saw him befriend such Holyrood greats as Clarke Gable, Cary Grant and many others, Gallishaw became a top consultant and writer for Paramount Pictures, Columbia Pictures, Metro-Goldwyn-Meyer and Universal Studios.

John Gallishaw started the famous Gallishaw School of Creative Writing at Cambridge, Massachussett's, which turned out many outstanding television and movie script-writers. On at least one occasion he collaborated with the famous F. Scott Fitzgerald on a filmscript based on one of Fitzgerald's books.

When World War I broke out, Gallishaw was a student at Harvard University. He quickly volunteered for the Canadian Forces, but later sought and received a discharge so he could join the Newfoundland Regiment. He expected this move would get him to the battlefront much quicker.

However, when authorities learned of his Harvard Background he was assigned to the War Office in London to keep the Regiment's records. Gallishaw wanted to see action so badly that he stowed away on the military transport ship taking the Newfoundland Regiment to Malta. At sea he turned himself in and volunteered for battle duty. His offer was accepted and he was assigned to B-Company. His first battlefield experience turned out to be his last. He took part in the evacuation of Gallipoli, where he was wounded and hospitalized.

After recovering from his wounds, he was shipped back to the United States and completed his studies at Harvard. Following this he became a lecturer at the same university.

When the U.S. entered the War in 1917, this fighting Newfoundlander volunteered for the American Forces. He saw action in France as a Commander of a Battalion, and was later assigned to American Intelligence.

In addition to his war-time experiences and Hollywood career, Gallishaw wrote five books, two of which were used in English courses in American Universities. In 1961 he returned to St. John's as a guest of Premier J. R. Smallwood, to attend the official opening of Memorial University.

Chapter V
Oddities

England had its Robin Hood and his merry men in Sherwood Forest. In Newfoundland we had Peter Kerrivan and his masterless men, and their Sherwood Forest was the Butterpots near Ferryland.

Unlike the folk-hero Robin Hood, who stole from the rich and gave to the poor, Peter Kerrivan and his masterless men robbed from the rich and the poor and kept it. Kerrivan, during the last half of the 18th century, formed the Society of Masterless Men, a resourceful band of outlaws which defied British law for more than twenty years.

The term masterless men was commonly used at the time to describe fishermen who had deserted their fishing vessels. However, only on the Southern Shore were the Masterless Men organized, and only there did they become a force to reckon with.

The Society chose a site near Ferryland known as the Butterpots for its camp. The site was perfectly suited for the purpose. It was nine miles from Ferryland Harbour, and gave the outlaws an ideal lookout over the entire area. It provided them with protection. With caribou herds nearby in excess of 5,000, there was no shortage of food.

Kerrivan became a masterless man after deserting the British Navy. He had been forced to serve with the navy after being captured by a press gang. Navy life in the 18th century was unbelievably cruel and brutal. The men were bullied by the officers, poorly fed and given very little clothing. They were often flogged or keel-hauled for the slightest breach of discipline.

Kerrivan deserted the Navy, and along with several companions fled to Newfoundland's Southern Shore where they founded the Society of Masterless Men. Kerrivan's bandits often raided communities along the shore, always returning to the safety of their Butterpot hideout. Their reputation spread and soon others came to join them.

Property owners complained to authorities, and the British made an all-out effort to end the outlaw activities. It took more than twenty years for the British to catch up with Kerrivan and his outlaws. They discovered the Butterpot hideout, and captured four of them. Kerrivan and most of his men escaped, but the four captured men were hanged from the yardarms of British ships anchored in Ferryland Harbour.

Strange Coffins — During the era of Sir William Coaker, a number of coffins were discovered at a place called Mockbeggar in Bonavista Bay. The discovery became one of the great mysteries of Bonavista. Some men digging out a canal at Mockbeggar during the early part of this century found a number of coffins containing the remains of men, women and children.

The mystery started when the coffins were opened and examined closely. It was observed that they were pegged and not nailed together and were made from a wood not found in Newfoundland.

Authorities were baffled. Immediate speculation was that they were French, because it was common knowledge that the French had been active in the fishery at Bonavista.

Some people refuted claims that the bodies were of French people. They noted that those in the coffins wore puritan-style clothing, and that the French did not bring women and children to Newfoundland when they frequented the fishing grounds.

Who then are the dead of Mockbeggar?

The coffins were buried below mud, which helped preserve them. Several homes were constructed over this unusual mud cemetery. Legend in the area has it that on a windy or stormy night you can hear the sound of singing in a foreign language coming from the burial area of Mockbeggar.

The Liar — Lying is not a practice generally encouraged, but there was a time in our history when a good liar saved the city of St. John's. This unusual episode from our past is recorded in the papers of Governor Sir James Wallace, and preserved at the Newfoundland Archives.

The year was 1776 and the Revolutionists were in control of France. St. John's was fast becoming a strategically important naval harbour. During this period a large French fleet appeared outside the narrows at St. John's Harbour. The fleet was under the command of Admiral Ritcery. St. John's was defended at the time by only three war vessels and about 600 soldiers. A boom and chain had been placed across the Narrows.

The French tried to assess the military strength of the City and decided, rather than risking a major military confrontation, to capture Bay Bulls — and to interrogate prisoners there about the defence, of St. John's.

The French easily captured Bay Bulls, along with many prisoners. Among those taken was a prisoner who appeared to be willing to cooperate with the French. He was taken on board the French ship *Jupiter* and questioned by French officers. He volunteered instructions on the correct route to St. John's by land, but described such hardships and hazards that the French were discouraged. He told them that there were 5,000 soldiers guarding St. John's, adding that a sea attack would be impossible because the harbour was fortified with two hundred cannons.

The French Admiral considered the information and decided against risking his fleet by attacking St. John's.

When Newfoundland Governor Wallace learned of how a liar had misled the French, he was delighted and told and retold the story for years after.

The First Concertina Player — A mob scene followed by an arrest accompanied the appearance of the first concertina in a small outport community in Newfoundland.

When Moses Bursey of Old Perlican was at the Labrador fishery, a friend gave him a musical instrument which was not too well-known around Newfoundland at that time. It was a concertina. Bursey had natural musical talent and quickly mastered the instrument.

When he returned to Old Perlican, word quickly spread about the amazing musical instrument and Bursey's talent.

Soon people began gathering at the Bursey home, and Bursey put on a show for them. The crowd became enthusistic, and suggested they march around the community with the music playing. Bursey obliged them and lead the crowd, playing all the while on the concertina *John Browne's Body*. Many people carried pans, pots and kettles and pounded on them as if they were drums.

This was the first band that ever played at Old Perlican and the first public demonstration ever witnessed there. When it was over Bursey went home, but the next morning he was summoned before the Magistrate to answer charges of leading a mob through the community.

There was a great deal of public interest in the trial, and if convicted Bursey was certain to get a term at Her Majesty's Penitentiary. Almost the whole community turned out for the proceedings. Some of those who had marched with him the night before testified against him. The Court found him guilty, and he was sentenced to 12 months in prison or a $250.00 fine. Bursey was unable to pay the fine and was prepared to go to jail.

Nevertheless, his friends in the community offered to pay it for him, but Bursey stood up and shouted, "No. Not one cent will I take." He added, "If I broke the law I will go to jail. But if I go to jail I go as an innocent man."

An uproar in the court followed Bursey's declaration, and the mob threatened that if Bursey went to jail there would be more trouble than ever previously witnessed in Old Perlican.

The Magistrate was not intimidated by the threats, but he was emotionally affected by the strong show of friendship and support for young Bursey. With tears in his eyes the Judge gave Bursey a brief lecture and an armful of books to read during the winter months. He then released him from serving any sentence or paying any fine.

Bouncing John Moxley — During the 19th century there was a place at Carbonear known as Moxley's Corner. The name has long disappeared from the community, but how it got its name is as intriguing and amazing a story as ever came out of Carbonear.

John Moxley was the victim of religious bigotry and the centre of one of the bitterest religious controversies in the history of Newfoundland. He had been born into the Roman Catholic faith, but as an adult he left the church. While he read the Protestant Bible and literature regularly, he never became a Protestant. His wife and children were Protestants and of course he never interfered with their religious beliefs or practices. He did, however, confide to friends that he wished to become one, but he feared some of the strong Irish Roman Catholics in Carbonear would kill him.

During March 1838, John Moxley was found dead. While the coroner determined he had died by suicide, the suspicion prevailed that he had been murdered. But the real controversy came when the family attempted to give him a proper burial. Neither Catholics nor Protestants wanted him.

At the Anglican graveyard, while the Minister prepared for funeral services, some members of the congregation gathered and tried to stop the grave diggers from opening the grave. Because of the interference, the diggers could only dig a few feet. Moxley was then laid to rest beneath three or four feet of clay.

Over the following weeks the major issue in the community was where Moxley should be buried. After all, he was not a Protestant, and he had left the Roman Catholic church. Several times small bands of protestors dug up Moxley's coffin and placed it outside the graveyard. When, as a solution to the problem, he was buried in the R.C. Cemetery, he was also dug up at night and thrown outside the graveyard. While the clergy was sympathetic and willing to allow proper burial for the deceased, the church members were not as charitable.

The controversy reached a peak when a band of men dug up Moxley's Coffin, which by then was falling apart, took the body out, stripped the clothing from it and tossed it over a cliff.

Outraged by this desecration, some true christians in the area — with the assistance of the coroner John Stark, who paid for a new coffin — in the darkness of night secretly buried the body once and for all in the woods near Carbonear.

While the Moxley coffin was being moved from the Protestant to the Catholic cemetery and then back again the Coroner had sent to authorities in St. John's asking for help in settling the dispute.

Moxley, meanwhile, left a wife and eight children. His estate, valued at $1,200.00, was supposed to go to the Crown. But because of the sympathy that developed for the family, the Crown allowed the full amount to go to the widow. For years after the place where Moxley was finally laid to rest was known as Moxley's Corner.

The Woman and the Cow — From 1696 onwards Bay Bulls was captured five times by the French. A dozen or more ships were sunk in Bay Bulls Harbour, the most famous being the British Man o' War *Sapphire,* which was excavated during the 1970s.

On one occasion at least the French did not act as conquerors. On January 26, 1705, about 400 French soldiers landed at Bay Bulls to mass for an attack on St. John's.

Instead of attacking the settlers there, the French pleaded with them for shelter, and were allowed to stay there for several nights in the homes and barns of the people.

In 1762 the Justice of the Peace there led volunteers from Bay Bulls over land to Petty Harbour, where they joined the schooners of Lord Colville in his successful effort to drive the French from St. John's.

During the see-saw battles between French and English, it wasn't always the men who showed courage. Following the French attack on Bay Bulls in September 1796, a lady resident stood up and defied the French.

The French attack came after they had been driven from St. John's. They took out their frustrations on the people of Bay Bulls. The people there fled into the woods for safety.

Upon returning to the smouldering ruins of Cottages and barns, one old woman was so outraged at the French who had stolen her only cow that she rowed alone out to the French commander's ship. She shouted at the French Admiral that she wanted her cow back. She made such a fuss, and the Admiral was so impressed by her courage, that he ordered his soldiers to load the cow on a raft and return it to her.

Battle of Fox Trap — The Battle of Fox Trap, in which the women of that community blubbered workers attempting to construct a railway through the community, may have been averted if the instigators had pronounced the word toll-gate correctly.

The seeds of discontent were set when two prominent city merchants discussed the proposed railway with two Irish settlers from Fox Trap who were visiting St. John's to sell their farm produce.

The merchants played on the known Irish dislike for the English by suggesting to them that the Queen was going to give Newfoundland to Canada, and that the Canadians would tax even the beds in which they slept. They insisted that the Canadians would place a toll-gate on the road to St. John's and no one would be allowed to get in or out. The only solution, the merchants argued, was for the people at Fox Trap to drive the railway workers out.

By the time the Irishmen got home to Fox Trap they were fighting mad. They told everyone they met of the Queen's plot to turn Newfoundland over to Canada. The Irishmen told their neighbours that the Canadians would put a tall goat (their understanding of the merchant's toll-gate) on the road to St. John's to prevent them from entering. This conjured up images among the people of Fox Trap of a giant ferocious goat, trained to attack poor farmers hoping for nothing more than to sell their produce in St. John's.

When Judge Prowse arrived the next day, he found the whole place in an uproar. It was August 4, 1880, and crowds had gathered to threaten the railway workers. The people believed that the red flannel danger flags used by the railway workers were Canadian flags, and they insisted that they be removed from Newfoundland soil.

Another amusing incident took place when Judge Prowse politely greeted the women of Fox Trap with the salutation, "Good Morning Ladies." Some women thought he was being sarcastic; one of them answered the Judge, saying, "We're not ladies, but we're probably as good as them that are."

The women then turned on the workers, stoning and blubbering them and chasing them out of the community.

Judge Prowse spent the next two days talking with each family, explaining to them that there would be no tall goat on the road to St. John's and the country was not being turned over to Canada. Things settled down, and soon the Battle of Fox Trap had ended.

Chapter VI
"Torbay — The Past Will Never Leave It."

My good friend, the late Captain Jack Dodd — the beloved old sea captain from Torbay — would have been shocked if someone had suggested to him that the first settler at Torbay was not Dennis McCarthy nor the Gosses nor the Codners. Captain Jack would likely have puffed on his pipe, nodded his head back and laughed loudly at the suggestion that Torbay was once known as Tarre Bay. He was a great and imaginative spinner of yarns. His stories, many of them told in his book *Wind In The rigging,* entertained thousands of Newfoundlanders and often attracted the attention of the media.

I remember on one occasion the Captain taking the local press to the top of a hill at Torbay. There he related the story of how a tall dead apple tree standing alone on the hill had gotten there. Captain Jack told reporters that it was brought here by the first settler at Torbay, Dennis McCarthy. McCarthy brought the tree over from Ireland and planted it on the hill near the site where he built his home. He nursed it, but after his death there was no one left to care for the only apple tree in Torbay. The tree died but remained standing on the site up until the late 1970s. It may still be there.

Captain Jack's story is an appealing piece of folklore and may have had some basis in fact, but it could not have been totally true. During the 16th and early 17th century Torbay was used mainly as a fishing station. Records as early as 1675 indicate there was no concentrated move to form a permanent settlement. Only three families lived there: John Cole and his wife, Edward Stocker and his wife and son, and James Corum. In addition to these people, there were two servants. (The

67

families owned two boats and six cattle, and in just one fishing season caught 350 quintals of fish.)

At that time the settlement was called Tarre Bay: a British Naval Captain, Sir John Berry, referred to it in his report to the British Government as Tarre Bay.

(Berry compiled a report to show how valuable the labour of permanent residents of Newfoundland was to British interests. The report came at a time when English merchants were trying to force permanent settlers out of Newfoundland. A plan had been devised to forcibly remove settlers and transport them to Jamaica. A St. John's resident John Downing led the successful battle to stop the merchants plan from being implemented, and his case was strengthened by the Berry report.)

While Torbay did not grow at a rapid pace, it was one of the earliest settlements in all Newfoundland. In 1675, between Torbay and Brigus in Conception Bay, there was only one other settlement — Harbour Main.

When the French captured Torbay in 1708, there were only four residents living there. The French had invaded all the communities from Cape St. Francis to Petty Harbour, and levied a ransom of 7,280 pounds sterling in return for not destroying property or taking prisoners. The Torbay settlers paid their portion of that ransom. By 1711 two new families had taken up residence there. They were the families of Abraham Barrett and Richard Sutton.

The Gosses, a common family name throughout Torbay today, first settled there in 1756 with the arrival of Solomon Gosse from Devon, England. Codner, another long-time prominent name throughout Torbay, took root there with the arrival of John Codner in 1774.

Historic Battle — Torbay gained recognition in world history, and has been honored by being declared a National Historic Site, because of its role in the Seven Years War between England and France. During that war there were many battles throughout Newfoundland, and in many cases the residents of the communities being attacked had to defend themselves.

Torbay was considered a valuable military strategic point, and gun batteries were set up to protect it. The batteries were set up at Cox Marsh on Torbay Road, on Piperstock Hill and one overlooking the bay. The Cox Marsh Battery had two cannons mounted on 18-pound carronades; the Piperstock Battery consisted of three cannons, covering the approach from Middle Cove; and the battery overlooking the bay, the largest one, had four six pounders and a guard house.

In the last battle fought in the Seven Years War, Colonel William Amherst used Torbay as the landing point to launch his attack on the French-held Signal Hill in St. John's. More than 800 soldiers took part in the battle, with help coming from a group of civilian fishermen known as Carter's Navy from the Southern Shore. Amherst defeated the French and drove them from the City.

Irish and English — When Torbay first began to grow it was mainly the Irish and the English that settled there. The Irish turned to the land to make there living, while the English turned to the sea. When the road from Torbay to Portugal Cove was built the workers on the project were not paid with money for their hard labour. Instead, the Government paid them with corn meal and molasses.

Pirates and Treasure — One of the many fascinating stories I recall hearing Captain Jack Dodd tell, as we sipped tea around his homemade wooden table in his home on the Bauline Line, was the story of the pirates of Treasure Cove. Treasure Cove is better known today as Tapper's Cove.

In that ominous, seaman-like tone of conversation that only Jack Dodd could deliver, he told of how the older residents of Torbay avoided Tapper's Cove at night because of the frequent apparations of a headless young boy and a phantom Newfoundland dog.

According to Dodd, the story had its beginning in the 17th century when pirates captured a Spanish galleon loaded with gold for the Spanish treasury and brought it to Tapper's Cove to loot. Most of the gold had been unloaded when another pirate ship sailed into Torbay and battled the first pirates for possession of the galleon. Having driven its original captors into the hills of Torbay, the attacking pirates removed the rest of the gold and then scuttled the galleon off the shore at Tapper's Cove.

According to legend the pirates dug an artificial steam through rock at the top of Treasure Cove. They made a wooden bottom for the stream, which somehow was connected to the place where the treasure was hidden. Before leaving Torbay they selected a young boy and his dog to guard the treasure. The superstitious pirates then cut off the boy's head and killed the dog in the belief their spirits would protect the buried treasure.

Finds Coin — This was just another colorful piece of Torbay folklore until the 1960's, when Captain Jack Dodd, fishing off Chair Cove, got his net tangled in something on the bottom of the ocean. When he managed to drag it on board he discovered a piece of fancily carved oak from the keel of a ship. Recalling the Treasure Cove story, the Captain began scouring the Tappers Cove area. He found a Spanish gold coin, dated 1784 with the inscription Carolus II, Dei Gratia, Hispas et Ind. Rex. Pictures of the coin and the oak log appeared in local papers. The Captain also found the old pirate well at the cliff on top of Tapper's Cove. There was a wooden bottom in the stream and the wood seemed to be foreign.

Although he continued his search, Captain Jack found nothing more, except the encouragement to continue the legend of the pirates of Treasure Cove.

A Real Pirate! — Captain Jack Dodd spent a life-time gathering and preserving the oral off-beat history of Torbay, and many of his colorful and often intriguing stories can be supported by historical documents. Captain Jack told many stories of pirates in Torbay, and history actually records at least one pirate who made his home in Torbay. He kept his wife and two sons there while he went on his many missions of piracy.

I am referring to Captain John Nutt, who deserted a British naval vessel in Newfoundland waters and turned to piracy. In three years he amassed a fortune, taking some of it back to England with him and burying some in secret hiding places. Among Nutt's first victims were a French ship, a Plymouth ship and a Flemish vessel. From these he went on to plunder the fishing fleets on the Grand Banks.

Although considered by authorities to be a blood-thirsty pirate, there was a humane side to John Nutt. He looked after his wife and family in Torbay; when other pirates attempted to attack and plunder the settlement at Ferryland, Nutt came to the rescue and fought them off. He paid his crew good wages and paid them on a regular basis.

In May, 1623, he wrote to Lt. Eliot in London, who had been ordered to arrest him. Nutt offered Eliot 300 pounds stirling in return for a pardon. Nutt upped the offer to 500 pounds and Eliot accepted. However, by the time Captain Nutt arrived in England, his period of grace had run out and he was arrested. The penalty for piracy at the time was to be tied to a stake at low tide, and as the tide came in the victim would have his throat cut and his body tossed into the sea.

Eliot was about to order the execution of the pirate from Torbay when Sir George Calvert, who later became Lord Baltimore, intervened. Calvert, remembering Nutt's valiant deed in defending the settlers at Ferryland, ordered Nutt's release and the arrest of Eliot.

Calvert said he had pardoned Nutt once and he would do it again. He commented, "I have no other end but to be graceful to a poor man that had been ready to do me and my associates courtesies in a plantation which we had begun in Newfoundland by defending us from others." Along with the pardon Calvert awarded Nutt 100 pounds sterling.

The Paintings — One of the attractions of Torbay is the series of five paintings by the Maltese artist Anthony Apap, which are on display at Holy Trinity Roman Catholic Church. Apap paintings hang in art galleries and churches in Canada, India, Australia and Malta. Those on display at Holy Trinity church depict The Holy Trinity, the Angel Gabriel informing Mary of the Conception of Jesus, the Raising of the Dead, The Last Supper and the Blessed Virgin Mary.

The paintings were donated to the Church by Charles Puglisevich, a native of Malta living in St. John's, on August 13, 1984. He made the donation to honour his 25th wedding anniversary.

Mr. Puglisevich brought in a professional from Ontario to frame the paintings before making the presentation to the church.

The Past — When you stand on the beach at Torbay on a sunny day, it's not difficult to imagine the days when pirates sought haven in this bay, or when Colonel Amherst led his troops ashore to launch the final battle of the Seven Years War.

While strolling through the meadows and green fields, the old folklore tales of Captain Jack Dodd spring to life in one's imagination: the tales of McCarthy's Apple Tree, the pirate ghosts of Tapper's Cove, the hidden treasure or sunken pirate ships in the bay. You could almost hear the singing of the Torbay men, content to toil to build roads for payment of only molasses and corn meal. Or imagine the Saturday night get-togethers that were so much a part of early life in the settlement of Torbay.

Yes sir! Captain Jack Dodd was right when he said, "No matter what the future brings for Torbay, the past will never leave it."

Chapter VII
Unusual War-time Stories

Newfoundlanders have displayed courage and bravery the world over. Whether on the high seas, tall mountains, the battle-front or at home, these Newfoundlanders have brought recognition for our province and pride to our people.

Perhaps the most unusual of these stories is that of Lt. Cyril Gardner of British Harbour. Gardner returned home from World War I with the German Iron Cross. This was unusual because it was presented to him by a German in the presence of a platoon of Germans at a time when we were at war with Germany.

Gardner was not a traitor; he did nothing to help the enemy. But he did perform a noble deed which earned him the respect and admiration of a 70-member German patrol.

Gardner's unit had been battling the German patrol when fog moved in over the battlefield resulting in the suspension of all fighting. Gardner, who spoke German, loaded his machine gun; under cover of darkness and fog he walked into the German camp speaking in German as he approached the sentries.

He captured the officers first, then the others surrendered. He disarmed the entire troop, ordered them to put their hands over their heads, and began marching them back towards allied lines.

As Gardner, escorting his prisoners, neared the allied camp, an English officer met them. After congratulating Gardner on his success, he prepared his gun for firing. He told Gardner he intended shooting the Germans on the spot. There was a brief moment of tension and fear among the Germans. Realizing the Englishman's intention, the Germans stepped backwards. At this point Lt. Gardner stepped in between the English officer and the enemy soldiers and said to the armed officer, "Put your gun back, or for the first German that falls I'll shoot you." The officer hesitated, then put his gun away and retreated.

The German Commanding Officer, who wore many medals for bravery, stepped forward. He saluted Gardner, and removing the Iron Cross from his own uniform, he pinned it on the chest of the Newfoundlander. The rest of the Germans applauded.

The Serbian Silver Medal — Henry G. Rideout is another Newfoundland hero of World War I. Rideout, a native of Pelley's Island, served with the Royal Navy on the Niobe. He was recommended for the Victoria Cross, but for some unexplained reason was never awarded that great honor.

He was, however, awarded two other medals for bravery. One of these was the Royal Serbian Silver Medal and the other was the 1914-1915 Star.

Actually, Rideout had been recommended for the Victoria Cross on two occasions. While serving on the Niobe, Rideout volunteered to join a landing party. He was 18 years old at the time. For three years he fought with this landing party in Serbia, often behind enemy lines.

During the occasion which earned him the Silver Medal, Rideout went behind enemy lines and cut German communication lines in several places. He also managed to destroy a number of enemy telephones and range finders.

For this mission he was awarded the Serbian Silver Medal by the Crown Prince of Serbia. At the same time a British Admiral recommended that Rideout be awarded the Victoria Cross.

Rideout returned to Newfoundland on July 17, 1919. When asked by reporters if he felt he would receive the Victoria Cross, he answered that he knew nothing about it except that he had been recommended.

The reporter who interviewed Rideout was Joey Smallwood, who later became Premier of Newfoundland. Rideout never did get the VC, and his name and deeds seem to have been lost in history.

The Sea Devil — During World War I, German Count Von Luckner earned the reputation throughout the world as 'The Sea Devil'. He earned it while in command of the German raider *Seadler,* which prior to the war was the American Clipper *'Pass'* of the Bahamas.

On one occasion the Sea Devil had taken several hundred prisoners on board. Among the prisoners being held was Captain B. G. Hooper from Lamaline, Newfoundland. After the War, Hooper became Marine Sueprintendent for Dominion Steel and Coal Corporation on Bell Island. He attributed most of his knowledge about the sea and being a sailor to the infamous Sea Devil.

In 1916 Hooper signed on the foreign-going three-masted schooner *Pearce.* The vessel was loading dry codfish and other cargo for Brazil. Just three weeks out of Halifax the *Pearce* was captured by the Sea Devil. The crew were taken prisoner on board the *Seadler,* and the Sea Devil ordered the sinking of the *Pearce.*

Hooper described the Sea Devil as a man of honor and lofty principles which he applied in war and peace. The prisoners lived in the ship's hold in conditions that were fairly good, and they were all treated well. They were allowed on deck when there was no action, but when the *Seadler* was raiding all prisoners were sent below and locked up.

He said discipline was rigid and they were obliged to work on deck. The Sea Devil insisted that every prisoner be paid and trained as well. Between January 24th and March 21st, 1917, the Sea Devil captured eight ships. He took all the crews and passengers prisoner before sinking them.

Because of the large number of prisoners the Sea Devil allowed many of them to return home. Among those set free was Captain Hooper, who was released at a Brazilian Port.

Teen-hero — A fifteen-year-old boy captured two German spies during World War I near the Marconi wireless station at Mount Pearl. Armed with a gun, Bernard Groves was doing sentry duty at the Marconi Station that night. A storm had covered the area with snow and it seemed like just another routine night for the teenager.

About a hundred yards from the station what appeared to be two banks of snow began to move.

Groves, thinking it was his buddies playing a joke on him, shouted, "Halt, who goes there?" He thought he'd give them a little scare by firing his rifle as well. At the sound of gunfire, the two men who were hiding beneath white camoflauge sheets suddenly stood up, throwing off the sheets and raising their hands in the air as a sign of surrender.

Groves had captured two German spies, who were attempting to destroy the Marconi station. The Germans were turned over to military authorities in St. John's, and Bernard Groves became a Newfoundland hero.

The Germans had been dropped off near Bay Bulls by a submarine under the command of Otto Oppelt, who had some very interesting pre-war connections with Newfoundland.

He was a powerfully-built German who was bought here by the Reid family, owners of the Newfoundland Railway, to work as their chauffeur. People in the city thought him a wreckless driver — he often drove through city streets at 10 miles per hour! He was also a famous wrestler who used the name 'Young Hackenschmit'.

A parade winding its way down Job Street, to celebrate the ending of World War I.

His most famous match took place at the CLB Armoury on the night of June 30th, 1911, when he fought a favourite named Young Olsen. Referee for that match was our famous

Newfoundland boxer Mike Shallow.

The wrestling bout thrilled the capacity audience with the two evenly-matched opponents battling for two and a half hours. It ended when doctors felt Olsen had been injured and was unable to continue. Oppelt was declared the winner. He returned to Germany when war broke out.

During the war his assignment was to carry out espionage and sink ships in the North Atlantic. Whenever he sank a ship he would always rescue the crew and passengers and land them safely on Newfoundland's south coast.

His knowledge of the Avalon peninsula enabled him to direct the sabateurs towards the Marconi station.

The Blue Puttees — The Newfoundland Patriotic Association has the distinction throughout the British Empire as having been the only non-government organization entrusted with recruiting and training soldiers. It had its beginning at a public meeting held at the CLB Armoury in St. John's on August 12th, 1914. The event was initiated by Governor Davidson following the outbreak of World War I, in an attempt to put together a military effort in Newfoundland to take part in the War.

A 50-member committee was set up at the meeting. The committee represented all religious and political viewpoints throughout Newfoundland. The organization became known as the Patriotic association, and was entrusted with the power to organize, equip and direct the military effort in Newfoundland.

Less than two weeks after that founding meeting a public appeal was made, requesting volunteers between the ages of 19 and 35 to enlist in the Newfoundland Regiment. The Newfoundlanders were given the same pay rate as that given to the Canadian military — one dollar per day. The response was encouraging. On the first day 74 signed up, and the number continued to grow. By September 2nd, 743 had enlisted.

The term of service was set for the duration of the war. But it was not to exceed one year, because it was felt the war would be over within a year.

The Patriotic Association then set up a training camp at Pleasantville. Tents to house the men were donated by local firms and private citizens. The Association also ordered local clothing firms to make uniforms for the Regiment. Due to the shortage of khaki material for making puttees, the troops were issued blue ones. The blue puttees became a mark of distinction for the first five hundred to go overseas. The Regiment became known as the Blue Puttees.

An offshot of the Patriotic Association was the Women's Patriotic Association, which by 1918 had distributed to the troops 30,000 pairs of socks, 1500 shirts, 6500 pairs of mitts and 40,000 scarves. The women also supplied cakes, dried salt cod, and hard bread to make fish and brewis. When pork fatback was not available they supplied fatty bacon. The women also sent more than a million cigarettes to the Newfoundland Regiment.

Meanwhile the Patriotic Association raised enough funds to purchase four planes for the British Air Force and 238 beds for a military hospital.

Margot Davis — During the Second World War the voice of Margot Davis was well-known throughout Newfoundland. Davis earned her reputation from a war-time radio broadcast from England, "Calling From Britain To Newfoundland." The popular program started under the direction of Maxwell Littlejohn, and was continued by Davis until her death.

The program originally broadcasted songs, music and poetry readings performed by Newfoundland servicemen stationed in Great Britain. But after the war, Davis expanded the program and sought out Newfoundlanders living in England to speak over the radio to their families and friends at home.

Davis helped thousands of young and lonely servicemen, and she became a legend throughout this province. She was born in St. John's and moved to England in 1934. She passed away in London in 1972.

Operation Overload — A Paradise man named Gilbert Lynch played a part in the Allied preparation for D-Day. On June 3rd, 1944, he was ordered by his commanding officer to go over to Normandy and destroy a floating jetty. Lynch recalled the assignment, saying, "We arrived in position by twilight and we blew it up. There was a lot of wood spread across the water, but Commander Phillips ordered us to leave."

A German U-Boat gave chase and followed Lynch's group back to Portsmouth. Lynch later said they knew they were clearing the wreckage for something special. On June 6th, 1944, they learned just how special that assignment was.

Lynch was not part of the first landing at Normandy on D-Day. but he arrived shortly after at a place called Golden Beach, along with 150 other soldiers, towing a pontoon bridge.

Prior to the invasion Lynch slept only in the daytime and worked all night. All night, under the cover of darkness, he and hundreds more worked on a secret project on the Isle of Wright, assembling a huge concrete bastion which was to become an artificial harbour after invasion.

Lynch recalled that there had been a great deal of stress in his unit because the men had no idea what was happening, yet they suspected something big was about to happen.

On June 8th, the artificial harbours he helped to build was in place. About a week later he saw King George VI, Winston Churchill, the Generals Eisenhower and Montgomery landing on the Normandy beach. For his part in the project Lynch was awarded the Silver Rosette. He was the only Newfoundlander in that special unit.

Americans Ignored Us! — Two American destroyers once stood idly by and watched a German U-boat sink two ships in American waters. Not only did the Americans do nothing to prevent the attack, but unbelievably accommodated a German request to move their destroyer back so they could have a good shot at the vessels.

One of the targets of U-53 was the *Stephano,* one of Newfoundland's well-known sealing vessels, which at the time was being used as a summertime passenger ship. The *Stephano* was the sistership of another Newfoundland vessel that met a tragic end — the *Florizel*.

The sinking occurred on October 9, 1916, about two miles off the Nantucket coast. The Germans simply approached the *Stephano* and fired four shots across her bow to bring her to a stop. Under the watchful eyes of the U.S. Navy they brought the vessel to a stop and ordered the Captain to instruct the 67 crewmembers and 97 passengers to abandon ship.

The Germans went onboard and looted the ship of all its valuables. As the drama at sea unfolded, 28 more American warships came to watch. But not one moved to prevent the German attack. The U.S. destroyer *Balch* took on all the passengers and crew from the *Stephano*. The Germans then fired 27 shots into the Newfoundland vessel's hull, seemingly with little affect. Lt. William Carey, interviewed later by the press, commented, "They did no damage, but they gave us some beautiful fireworks to gaze at."

The U-boat then fired another torpedo which broke the ship in two, causing her to sink quickly. Lt. Carey commented, "There being nothing else to do, we waved good-bye to the Germans and shaped our course for Newport."

Although the U.S. was neutral at the time, critics in that country claimed the German action was illegal. Some American lawyers argued the sub should have been interned in an American port before she could do any damage. Another critic of the U.S. Navy at that time was George Wallace of Freeport, New York, who asked, "What kind of officers were in charge of these war vessels. Even if the passengers had not been Americans, any of our old-time sea worthies would have rushed to the rescue in the cause of common humanity."

U-Boat Action — It's surprising how much enemy action did take place in Newfoundland or near Newfoundland during both World Wars. Much of this has been covered in my other books. However, a little-known story is the one involving the sinking of the S.S. *Geraldine Mary* by a German U-boat on August 4, 1940.

The *Geraldine Mary* was owned by the Anglo-Newfoundland Development Co. Ltd., and was being used to transport newsprint from Newfoundland.

In consideration of the heavy ice which sometimes blocks access to Newfoundland ports, the vessel was equipped with especially designed bows for ice-breaking. In addition to space for the officers and crew, the vessel had six staterooms that could accommodate 12 passengers.

On July 19, 1940, the *Geraldine* left Botwood to join a convoy out of Halifax on its way to the United Kingdom. The convoy, which was code-named HX60 was unknowingly sailing straight into the path of three German U-boats. They had orders to attack all north-American convoys.

U-boat 52, under the command of Otto Salman, on August 4 upped periscope and slammed a salvo of torpedos into the Newfoundland cargo ship. The blasts broke the ship in two and sent her to the bottom. Fortunately, only one passenger was lost. He was H. C. Thompson of Mortier Bay. One of the passengers on the *Geraldine* was a Miss Gordon, who was going to London to marry Derek Bowring. At the time Bowring was serving in the 166th Nfld. Regiment.

The Ocean Empire — Another merchant ship, the *Ocean Empire,* was attacked by German U-boats near Cape Race. The vessel was armed with a spitfire plane, that could be launched from the ship by a catapult. It was travelling with a convoy when the Germans attacked. The *Ocean Empire* left the convoy and headed for Cape Race with the U-boat following. The chase continued into the next day when a heavy fog settled over the area. Whether or not the captain of the *Empire* beached the ship to rid himself of the shadowing submarine is not known. However, nearly half the ship was left on the rocks at Long Point, near the radio beacon at Cape Race.

As the fog lifted, two vessels appeared on the scene, one to try and refloat her and the other to destroy her if the first ship failed. The *Empire* was towed from the rocks. She was being kept afloat by air trapped beneath the forward hatches. Just off Calvert, on the Avalon Peninsula, these hatches gave out and the ship went down.

The Atlantic Charter Not Signed[1] — On Saturday, August 9, 1941, the Atlantic Charter was agreed upon between President F. D. Roosevelt of the United States and Prime Minister Winston Churchill of England. I use the term agreed upon, because contrary to popular belief the agreement was never signed. During the four-day meeting the Charter was revised many times; and when verbal approval had been reached, it was telegraphed to London and Washington for study. Both Governments then gave approval to the document known as the Atlantic Charter.

It wasn't until after the historic meeting that the world learned of the location of this top-secret meeting. The meeting itself was to be kept secret; however, three days before it took place, a radio station in Cincinatti, Ohio, reported that

Washington sources were saying that the President was to meet Churchill somewhere in the Atlantic.

President F. D. Roosevelt boarding the British Warship *Prince of Wales* which carried British Prime Minister Winston Churchill. Photo taken at Placentia Bay, Nfld., 1942. 1942. Courtesy American Legion, St. John's, Nfld.

The purpose of the meeting was not known by the public. It was not until six days after Churchill returned to England that he told of his meeting with Roosevelt, held somewhere in the north Atlantic.

Churchill arrived in Placentia Bay on the warship *Prince of Wales* during the early morning of August 9th. The vessel had recently undergone repairs after taking part in the famous battle with the *Bismark*. Roosevelt, aboard the cruiser *Augusta* and accompanied by a flotilla of warships, was already awaiting Churchill.

As the two warships drew abreast the President and Prime Minister saluted each other. The Royal Marine Band played the "Star Spangled Banner" while the American band played "God Save The King."

On the final night of the meeting there were some anxious moments in St. John's. An unidentified aircraft suddenly approached the city, which was blacked out in accordance with war-time regulations. Anti-aircraft guns protecting the city were alerted and ready to fire when the identity of the plane was determined. It was Lord Beaverbrook.

Search lights went out and an all-clear sounded. Beaverbrook was on his way to the secret meeting but had no way of getting to Placentia. The Newfoundland Railway made special arrangements for a train to take Beaverbrook to Argentia. Almost everybody on Churchill's ship was asleep when he arrived at 5 a.m. the next morning. He joined the meetings with the two world leaders and then returned by train to St. John's. From there he took an evening flight to Washington to continue discussions on behalf of Churchill and Roosevelt.

Churchill, speaking later to the British Nation and describing the historic event, said, "In a spacious landlocked bay which reminded me of the west coast of Scotland, powerful American warships, protected by a strong flotilla, and far-reaching aircraft awaited our arrival, and as it were, stretched out a hand to help us in . . ."

The Atlantic Charter was meant to prevent future wars and was a forerunner of the United Nations.

German Military in Newfoundland — The only place in North America where the Germans during the Second World War were able to land and establish an on-land installation was on the Northern Labrador coast. Evidence discovered at the site showed the Germans had set up an automatic weather station.

This discovery was made by Canadian historian M. Alex Douglas of the Department of National Defence and a German industrialist named Franz Selinger.

The information which led to the discovery was gathered from the log book and pictures taken from a captured German submarine. These records indicated that a great weather station had been transported across the Atlantic in a sub and taken to shore by the crew at Martin's Bay, 32 kilometers south of Cape Chidley. The records also revealed that the sub had successfully evaded three attacks by the Canadian Coast Guard.

The Germans carried the station ashore using a rubber raft, then scaled a 60 meter cliff, managing to complete the work in one day. The station operated for three months before the batteries gave out. However, while in operation the station provided the Germans with knowledge of the weather patterns affecting the North Atlantic shipping lanes and Europe.

Evidence gathered at the site showed that at some point the station had been discovered and smashed by unknown agents. When the research team arrived at the site, they found it strewn with barrel-like weather cannisters. It had not been systematically disassembled, but the wires had been cut and one of the cannisters was missing. The Germans had printed on all the cannisters the title 'Canadian Weather Service.'

The recovered station is the property of the Newfoundland Government but was sent to Museum Canada in Ottawa for restoration and display.

The Edmund B. Alexander — The American troopship *Edmund B. Alexander* arrived in St. John's on January 30th, 1941, carrying the first American troops for service in Newfoundland. The large troopship carried 2,000 servicemen. They were to man the U.S. base at Pleasantville, then called Fort Pepperrell. Over the following twenty years more than 90,000 American servicemen were stationed on American bases throughout Newfoundland.

The Edmund B. Alexander, the American Troop Ship that brought the first American soldiers to St. John's in 1942. (photo courtesy American Legion, St. John's, Nfld.)

The Alexander was built in Belfast, Ireland in 1905, and at 21,000 tons was the largest ship ever to enter port at St. John's up to that time.

Top Secret — Early one morning in 1942 the military in St. John's were convinced that an invasion of Newfoundland by the German Navy had started. An alarm was raised and all military personnel were placed on alert. The reaction was sparked by the sound of gunfire and explosions, and by fire visible in the skies near Cuckhold's Cove just east of St. John's Harbour.

While the military in the city scrambled to prepare for the attack, they received an urgent call from the Commander of U.S. Forces at Argentia. He told them there was no need to be concerned. The Commander stated that a top-secret weapon had been developed at Argentia and was at that very moment being tested near Cuckhold's Cove.

When the local media questioned the military the following day about sounding of the alarm, they were told the alarm had been set off accidentally by a short circuit. That answer failed to satisfy residents in the area, who told of being awakened by terrifying explosions and seeing the sky lit up by bursts of flame. The military explained this away by claiming it was something caused by an electrical storm.

Following the war many top-secret documents were made public and among them were those that concerned the incident at Cuckhold's Cove. It seems that in 1942 the U.S. was well-aware that an invasion of Europe was inevitable. Their scientists had developed a weapon which later helped to defeat Germany, and they were looking for a suitable place to test it.

Keeping in mind the lesson of Dieppe and the knowledge of intended landings, they were seeking some method by which troops could gain a foothold on a beach head without experiencing heavy casualties. In response to the dilemma the Americans came up with the famous rocket-firing landing-craft, which at the time was regarded as one of the most effective weapons in warfare. The Americans selected the rough and sometimes stormy coastline near Cuckhold's Cove as the place to test this top-secret weapon.

The weapon was towed to Argentia, where Newfoundland workmen under the supervision of U.S. military technicians assembled it. To test the unknown qualities of the rocket-firing landing-craft, it was decided to sail direct from Argentia to the rendezvous point, which was set at about one mile off the coast of Cuckhold's Cove. For tactical and security reasons, the trial run was scheduled for early morning, with stormy weather approximating battle conditions.

The experiment was a success and the new weapon approved. It proved its usefulness in the D-Day landings at Normandy Beach.

Britain's Treasury in St. John's Harbour — In July 1940, two ships moored in St. John's harbour were carrying a top-secret cargo, the contents of which were not revealed until after World War II. The cargo was a quarter of a billion dollars, which belonged to the British Treasury.

In 1940 Prime Minister Winston Churchill considered the likelihood of a German invasion in England all but certain. He discussed this with his cabinet, and a decision was made to have a major part of the British treasury sent to Canada for safe keeping. If England did fall, the British had a secret plan to carry on the war from Canada.

Within ten days, a fortune of several billion dollars in gold and securities was ready for transportation to Canada. The first shipment went out successfully on the British cruiser *Emerald.* On July 8th the remainder of the valuable cargo left British ports in five ships, altogether carrying almost two billion dollars in gold.

Four destroyers accompanied the fleet until they were 20 miles from England, out of reach of the German Air Force. Although targets for U-boats, they were all capable of travelling at a high speed.

When the fleet passed through Newfoundland waters, a ship called the *Batory* developed engine trouble. The Admiral in charge decided that rather than slow down the fleet, making it an easy target for German U-boats, he would send the *Batory* to St. John's for repairs. He assigned the *Bonaventure* to escort her.

On the *Bonaventure* and *Batory* combined there was a quarter of a billion dollars; and when they ran into a heavy fog as they neared St. John's, the Vice-Admiral on the *Bonaventure* expressed grave concern. They reduced speed and made it to St. John's safely.

At St. John's the *Batory* was repaired and went on to rejoin the treasure fleet at Halifax. From there a heavily-guarded train took the fortune to Montreal, where it was placed in the basement of the 24 story Sun-Life Assurance Building.

The secret of the *Batory* and *Bonaventure's* cargo was perhaps the best-kept secret of World War II in Newfoundland. Not even the highest Government officials here were aware of it.

Chapter VIII
Violent Indians

The history of the Beothuks in Newfoundland doesn't compare in any way with the violent background of most North American Indian tribes. Although the Beothuks were generally peaceful, there were isolated incidents of extreme violence in their past.

Captain Buchan — Captain David Buchan had encounters with the Beothuks and kept a diary. It was from this diary that we learn of one of the most violent incidents in the history of the Beothuks.

Captain Buchan lead a group of British marines up the Exploits River to seek out the Beothuk Indians. Part way up the river, the group came upon a small Indian village. Buchan wrote in his diary, "I strictly charged my men to avoid every impropriety and to be especially guarded in their behavior towards the women."

He added, "My first object was to remove their fears and inspire confidence in us which was soon accomplished by our shaking hands and showing every friendly disposition." According to Buchan, once a peaceful attitude prevailed at the campsite the Indians showed surprise and interest in the way the white men were dressed.

They treated Buchan and his men to a feast of venison and other Indian dishes. Gifts were exchanged; but then Buchan had great difficulty in communicating to them that he was going back to his ship to get some more gifts for them. Corp. Jim Butler and Private Tom Britland volunteered to remain with the Indians. By the same token several Beothuks went with Buchan and his men down the Exploits.

When they returned with the gifts, a horrible site greeted them. Buchan found Butler and Britland stretched out on the ice with their heads cut off. Why the Indians had suddenly turned violent remained a mystery until a few years later when a Beothuk woman was captured by some white men. She was from the tribe that had killed Buchan's men. She explained that one of the Indians who accompanied Buchan down the Exploits had deserted the white men because he feared they were going to bring back more men and attack the Indian camp. He returned to the camp and told the others what he expected. The Beothuks turned on the two white men in camp and killed them. Then they fled into the interior of the island.

Scalped — The world-famous Sir Joseph Banks, who gained his place in world history as a Botanist, recorded an interesting item regarding the Beothuks. Banks noted in his diary that he had seen the face and scalp of a man which had been taken off by Beothuk Indians.

According to Banks, the victim ws a man named Frye. While swimming out to his boat, he was shot and killed by Indians with arrows. The Indians went beyond the traditional scalping and actually cut off the face of the man as well. They carried the scalp with them and dropped it while being chased by white men. Banks wrote that the Beothuks had skinned the victim's face right down to his upper lip.

There was a population of about 500 Beothuks in Newfoundland at the time of Bank's visit, and they were continually at war with the white population. Sometimes the white men plundered Indian camps and took their belongings, which often included a mixture of eggs and the hair from deer and bears, a mixture similar to mortar.

Banks was impressed by the archery skills of the Beothuks. He noted that they could take four arrows, put one on the bowstring and clutch the other three in the hand that held the bow. Thus they could shoot all four in rapid succession.

Bow-Arrow Attack — During 1762 a shipsmaster named Scott landed with his crew at Exploits (then called Burnt Island). They constructed a fort at the mouth of the Exploits River. Some days later they got their first glimpse of the Beothuk Indians. A group of Indians came within a few hundred yards of the fort and stopped.

Scott was curious about their behaviour and decided to investigate. He recruited several volunteers; completely un-armed they went out to greet the Indians. Scott bravely walked up to the Indians and extended his hand as a sign of welcome.

One of the Beothuks responded by putting his arm around Scott's neck; suddenly another Indian plunged a knife into Scotts back. This was followed by a bow and arrow attack upon the defenceless men. The shower of arrows killed five men; the others safely reached the fort.

The survivors took one of the bodies to St. John's, with the arrows still in it, to show authorities. Meanwhile the victims were buried on the hill overlooking Little Harbour. The mounds of turf which cover the graves are still visible.

In a little church cemetery nearby is the body of John Peyton, the man who had frequent contacts with the Beothuks and who took the Indian girl Shanawdithit into his house as a servant. There is a rock on the shore in front of the former Peyton House where Peyton carved his initials, which are still clearly visible.

Another Side — For Mark Young at Twillingate in 1715, Christmas was a real frontier-type one. It was a severe winter, and Mark did not have enough food to last until spring. Food was scarce because some Indians had destroyed nearly half of Mark's small potato patch during the fall. Early frost then took its toll on the other vegetables. Wild game was scarce.

Just before dawn on Christmas Eve, Mark was tramping through the wood on his snow shoes, setting rabbit slips. The noises of the woods and sharp snapping of the frost may have made a more nervous man shiver, but Mark was well-used to travelling about alone.

Suddenly, along with the usual sounds there came a faint moan which stopped him in his tracks. A caribou in some Indian trap, he thought. Moving cautiously in the direction of the sound, he came upon a mound of snow, from which was sticking the arm of an Indian youth.

Fearful at first of some Indian trick, Mark got his gun ready. But he soon learned it was no trick; he could plainly see that the boy was perishing. Without hesitation he scraped the snow from the almost lifeless body and hoisted it on his back. There he started for his cabin.

When he arrived, he placed the boy in a warm bed and covered him with his warmest deer skins. Mark managed to get a few spoonfuls of venison soup between the boy's almost purple lips, and soon had the satisfaction of seeing him sleeping peacefully.

When darkness fell Mark went outside to his woodpile to gather wood for the evening. Then he was suddenly jumped and taken prisoner by three Indians. They bound his arms and feet and took him inside the cabin.

While they were searching the cabin for things to steal, the commotion woke the boy, who started to cry. With a shout of joy, one of the Indians threw his arms around the boy. It was his father.

There was a great deal of excitement among the Indians as they waved their arms and pointed towards Mark. There was a picture on the table of Christ in the manger. One of the Indians pointed to it, saying "Kismas" several times. They then replaced the things they had stolen and cut Mark free. Bowing low as they left the cabin, each Indian said to Mark, 'Kismas, good man.'

They retreated silently, leaving Mark alone with his fire. He was glad indeed that he had been able to breathe a little of the Christmas spirit into the hearts of these Indians.

Chapter IX
Bits n' Pieces About St. John's

One of the many colourful characters of old St. John's was a west-ender named Bernard Walsh. Walsh had little formal education and lacked the desire to work for a living. Yet he possesed a native shrewdness which amused and sometimes surprised the people of the city. While walking along Water Street one April Fool's Day, he was stopped by Ned Noonan, one of the well-known sportsmen of the day. "Bernard," said Noonan, "take a note down to Jimmie Baird for me, like a good fellow. It's something important, so make sure he gets it."

"Sure, I'll be glad to oblige, Mr. Noonan," Walsh replied.

Noonan quickly penned the note and passed it to Bernard in an envelope, which in his haste he forgot to seal. Bernard placed it in his pocket and ambled down Water Street until he was out of sight. He then opened the envelope and read the message. Taking a pencil from his pocket he added a line to it, put it back in the envelope, and continued on to Baird's.

It took Bernard all afternoon to make the rounds of every tavern and public house on Water Street, where he duly presented the note. By 6:00 p.m. he was discovered propped up against a wall fast asleep, still clutching the crumpled envelope. When opened it revealed the following message: "Send the fool further" to which Walsh had added, "and give him a drink."

Bavarian Ale — During the early days of the brewing industry in St. John's, one of the most popular ales in the city was Bavarian Ale. It was made by Lindbert's Brewery. The

Government of the day ruled the beverage to be an alcoholic drink more for tax purposes than for any commitment to temperance.

The company attempted to show that it was not intoxicating. An employee named Tom Murdock made a statement that he had many times drank several quarts of the delicious beverage without becoming in the least intoxicated. The company, however, lost its case; but Murdock was remembered for posterity in the following lines:

When Tom Murdock is dead and in his grave,
For Bavarian Beer he will not crave,
But on his tombstone will be wrote
Many's a gallon went down his throat.

Two Old Characters — Two Irish characters of old St. John's named Kelley and Hartery each operated a cab service in the City during the early 1900's. They both liked to drink and often played cards. They also both had a stubborn streak which often delighted and amused their friends and the people of St. John's.

One such encounter started in a Water Street Saloon in the year 1901. While enjoying a few ales and some whiskey, Kelley challenged Hartery to a game of cards. They agreed that following the game they would exchange horses and the loser would pay the winner five dollars. Hartery won, and decided to let Kelley keep the five dollars because he owed him that anyway. Hartery also reasoned that since he owned a better horse than Kelly, there would be no advantage in making the swap.

In true Irish fashion they shook hands and walked out of the saloon arm in arm. A short while later they were at Kelly's house, which was in the west end of St. John's. A few more drinks were had, and Kelley challenged Hartery to another game of cards. But this time the loser would pay the winner ten dollars in addition to swapping horses.

Well, this time Kelley won; but he wasn't as big-hearted as Hartery had been just hours earlier. He took the money and locked Hartery's horse in his barn. He then hitched his old nag to Hartery's cart. But Hartery refused to accept Kelley's horse.

An argument erupted which ended with Kelley going inside and going to bed. Meanwhile, Hartery refused to take the old nag, and couldn't get his own horse from Kelley's locked barn. So he walked home, leaving the old nag standing in the middle of the road. Early the next morning both men were arrested for abandoning the horse. Hartery was acquitted, but Kelley was fined ten dollars. It was some time before the two began speaking to each other; it came about over a game of cards, with just money this time and no horses for the prize.

The Band Master — When the Atlantic Cable was brought ashore from the *Great Eastern* at Heart's Content in 1866, Professor David Bennett's Band was there leading the welcome. When the corner stone for the Hospital for Mental and Nervous Diseases was laid on July 27, 1853, Professor Bennett's Band supplied the music.

Bennett's famous band also supplied music for the first passenger trip on the Reid Newfoundland railway. As a matter of fact, the Bennett Band was perhaps the most famous one in all Newfoundland from the 1830's to the 1890's. Bennett, an expert musician and band leader, was a professor of music at St. Bonaventure's College in St. John's. One of his most famous students was another great man of music, Sir Charles Hutton.

Bennett received his musical training in the Royal Newfoundland Company; he became a familiar and popular Newfoundland figure as leader of many bands. During the 19th century most organizations and societies had their own bands. Bennett's first band was the one formed by the Total Abstinence Society. He lead that band for 20 years. During his career he also led the band of the Queen's Own Volunteer's.

In 1863 Bishop Mullock appointed Bennett to the position of music professor at St. Bonaventure's College. When the Star of the Sea was formed, he organized and led its first band. His bands played for every Newfoundland Governor from Prescott, 1836, to Maxse, 1862. He played for the visit of His Royal Highness Prince Henry of the Netherlands in 1845, and His Royal Highness the Prince of Wales (later King Edward VII) when he came to St. John's in 1860.

He was present at many of the history-making events of the 19th century. He played for the fencing of the Roman Catholic Basilica Grounds as well as for the digging of the foundation. Citizens' groups of all religious backgrounds combined to carry stone for the Basilica, and once again they were inspired by Bennett's Band.

Bennett also played for the first stone hauled for St. Patricks' Church, and the consecrations of the new churchs at Blackhead, Ferryland and Torbay. For 25 years he supplied music for the first mass on Christmas morning at the Basilica.

When the Anglican Church Lads Brigade was formed, Bennett organized and provided musical instruction for their first band. During his lifetime Bennett received many awards, including the Medal of Merit from the British Army for his outstanding musical service to the military.

Our First Newspaper — Newfoundland newspapers did not always enjoy the freedom of the press that is today a basic right. As a matter of fact, there was a time when every word written for publication in a Newfoundland newspaper had to be screened and approved by censors before being published. The censors were the Magistrates of Saint John, N.B.

The newspaper first subjected to this policy was Newfound-founded in 1807 by John Ryan, one of a band of U.S. loyalists.

After the Declaration of Independence he gave up his property to seek a new life under the British flag. At first he settled at New Brunswick, there becoming the King's printer and operating out of Saint John.

However, when the capital of New Brunswick was moved to Fredricton, in disgust Ryan moved to Newfoundland. At the time of his arrival in St. John's, there were strict controls on settlement. In order to build a home or operate a business one had to obtain permission from the Government. A newspaper was looked upon as a menace, a dangerous innovation.

Ryan succeeded in getting his paper off the ground because he made a favourable impression on the merchants of the city, who took his cause to the Governor. It was Governor Erasmus Gower who gave permission for the *Royal Gazette* to publish, and it was Gower who set down the unusual but stringent regulations governing publication.

He demanded that Ryan post a 200 pound stirling bond with the court, and that before each publication he submit his material to the Magistrates in St. John's for censorship. In addition, the Governor forbade Ryan to build his house on Water Street because that area was reserved for people involved in the fishery.

Ryan brought his presses from New Brunswick and began publishing his *Royal Gazette* on August 27, 1807. The population of St. John's in that year was 6,000.

The Wood Haul — During the mid 19th century, the greatest annual event in the city of St. John's was the famous wood haul for the R.C. Cathedral and the Presentation convent. There was always a great demonstration of public spirit, with people from all denominations taking part. Prominent among the wood haulers were the great sealing skippers and their crews.

Those who could afford to do so purchased loads of wood from the farmers. The order was that nothing but large spruce would be accepted. The great majority took their dogs and sleds, three or four men to each team, and headed for the country. When they had sufficient wood to fill the great drays they started loading up. These drays were made of 8 inch square timber, with three runners bolted together with cross bars, sufficient to stand the great weight of 1800 to 2000 sticks.

When all the loads in the different parts of the town were built up and well secured, the hauling hawsers, which were donated for use by the merchants and sealing masters, were placed in a position for the grand tow. Two six-inch ice liners, used for moving the sealing vessels, were fastened to each load. They were needed to withstand the tremendous pulling of 2,000 men.

There were 3 guys of strong rope, with 25 men on each side — picked men, who knew what to do to prevent the loads from toppling over. There was also a large steering stick built into each load, with some seven or eight specially selected men on hand to guide the huge mass of wood along the line of road. When all was ready the order to man the ropes thundered out. Then off they would go, headed by Bennett's Band and others, which provided some good old-time music and shanty songs.

When the loads were started, the ship's masters issued their orders in nautical terms. This was always their mode of expression; they neither knew nor cared for any other. When all had arrived at the cathedral grounds, each crew would un-load its own dray and stow the wood away. After that they would look after the hawser's chains and ropes to see they got back to their owners.

When the haul was finished, the men returned to the different hotels or the hospitable residences of the famous sealing masters. There they discussed the events of the day, with a great deal of argument over who had the largest load.

Graveyards! — The only religion permitted religious free-dom in Newfoundland during the period from the arrival of Sir Humphrey Gilbert to the end of the 18th century was the Church of England. Once a Church of England parish had been established in St. John's, a protestant graveyard was opened. It was located at the site of the present Anglican Cathedral, opposite the Court House on Duckworth Street.

The Anglican Church viewed Newfoundland as a mission-ary parish. All the bodies and souls of all the inhabitants were in theory the property of the Church. Even when other religions developed here, all faiths were expected to bury their dead at the Church of England cemetery, and no religious ceremony was complete without the sanctions of the Angli-can clergy. Even under the popular RC Bishop Louis O'Don-nel, this double-rite system continued.

It meant that baptism, marriage and burial services had to be performed by an Anglican priest in addition to the Ro-man Catholic priest. When a royal proclamation was issued in 1784 giving freedom of worship to all, the double-rite prac-tice continued in Newfoundland. Roman Catholics often de-fied the local law and would wait until nightfall to bring their dead into the cemetery to conduct their own services.

The Roman Catholics pressured the Newfoundland gover-nors to allow them to have their own graveyard and conduct their own services. They were told that they could have their own cemetery, but until one was found they would have to continue to use the Protestant cemetery and the Anglican clergy.

The Catholics established a cemetery of their own on a par-cel of land at Long's Hill. The first person buried there was a Mrs. John Butt, who at the age of 94 was the oldest person in St. John's when she died in 1784. Her remains were removed from the Anglican graveyard and interred at Long's Hill around 1811, the year the RC cemetery opened.

Tombstones were rarely used in St. John's before the 1820's, but over the following decade many were imported from Waterford, Ireland, a tradition which became widespread. Near the end of the 19th century graves at Long's Hill were moved to make room for road construction and also for sanitary reasons. The bodies were transferred to Mount Carmel and Belvedere Cemeteries.

Torbay Airport — The first aircraft landing at Torbay Airport took place on October 18, 1941, at a time when the runways were still under construction. While workmen laboured, three U.S. Air Force B-17 bombers circled the unfinished airfield several times as a signal they wished to land.

The runways were evacuated and the three bombers landed safely. Canadian officials were annoyed because the landings were a danger to construction workers as well as the crews of the airplanes.

Another and more dramatic landing took place on October 31, 1941, when severe weather conditions forced a British Overseas Airways Liberator AM*262 to make a forced landing. The aircraft was on a return trip from Scotland to Gander, with fifteen passengers and five crew members.

By the time the aircraft had passed the point of no return an earlier snowstorm had worsened, making a landing in Gander impossible. The bad weather was being experienced all along the eastern seaboard, thus preventing a landing anywhere east of Montreal. In desperation the pilot sought permission to land at Torbay where only one of the two runways was near completion. Authorities felt the situation was serious enough to warrant the landing, and instructions were given to prepare for it.

The British aircraft landed safely with the permission of RCAF headquarters in St. John's. Because permission had been given to land, it was recorded as the first official landing at Torbay Airport.

There was no instrument landing-aids at the airport at that time. Radio station VONF, which was usually off the air at that time of day, was asked to remain on air and was used by the aircraft as a homing Beacon. The aircraft landed with minor damage to its nose wheel. The first Air Canada flight to arrive at Torbay Airport was a Lockheed Lodestar which arrived on May 1, 1942.

Chapter X
Gun Runners & Privateers

Off the coast near Elliston, Trinity Bay, lies the wreck of a ship named the *Thomas Gould Croff*. The cargo of guns and ammunition that went down with her was destined for the Southern United States during the American Civil War. The ship had set sail from Valentia, Ireland, destined for Charleston, where Confederate forces anxiously awaited the delivery of the much-needed guns and ammunition.

The vessel had to run the gauntlet of the Northern blockade of Southern ports, and the Captain chose to sail through the Straits of Belle Isle to evade the Yankees. He felt that this course would shorten his trip as well. But the Captain was not familiar with northern Newfoundland waters. About 60 miles east of Cape Bonavista the ship ran into heavy ice, which forced the Captain to turn south.

The trouble continued. The vessel was continually bumped and battered by the ice pans; finally she became so badly damaged she had to be abandoned.

The Captain and crew escaped in a large dory and watched as the valuable cargo went to the bottom. The dory drifted into Elliston. By the time they got to land most of the men were frost-bitten, and in some cases gangarene had set in. They were so far gone that all hands except the Captain and two crewmen soon died.

The dead men from the gun-running vessel were buried at the Methodist cemetery at Elliston. The three survivors were sent home.

Privateers — During the late 18th century American privateers terrorized Newfoundland fishermen and shipowners. Many Newfoundland-owned vessels were attacked and captured by the privateers, but the Americans met their match when they moved into St. Mary's Bay.

It was the year 1782 when the Yankee privateer *Hazard*, under the command of Captain Hugh Elmes, was attacking ships near St. Mary's Bay. The *Hazard* was equipped with six guns and had a crew of 24. It followed and captured a ship that had left St. Mary's Bay heading for Trepassey. The privateers caught up with it at Cape English; and after plundering that vessel went to North Harbour, where they captured three more.

When word of this reached St. Mary's Bay the fishermen decided that rather than send to St. John's for military help they would handle the privateers themselves. The firm of Pinney and Frampton made a boat available to the fishermen, who collected guns from other ships in the harbour and mounted them on the boat.

Twenty two men volunteered to man the St. Mary's warship, and they set out to battle the Yankee privateers. On September 16th they caught up with the *Hazard*. The Yanks were no match for the St. Mary's baymen, who captured them and took control of their ship.

Among the captured privateers was a man named John Dart who had lived for awhile at Trepassey. The prisoners were taken to St. John's. The Governor was so delighted with the success of the St. Mary's baymen that he allowed them to keep the privateer vessel and its cargo.

Newfoundland Defeats U.S. — During the late 18th century when Canada was invaded by the United States, she fought off the invasion with a major part being played by volunteers from Newfoundland.

With a force of only 180, Newfoundland's contribution in manpower seemed small; but our troops arrived on the scene when a feather could have turned the scale. Canada's position was critical. It was under attack by two American armies and two naval vessels. Besides those in the fort at Chambly and St. John there were less than 200 soldiers in all Canada. It was under these circumstances that Captain Colin Campbell decided to go to Newfoundland for reinforcements. Newfoundland was only a fishing station at the time with a population of 9,000, 1,500 of these living in St. John's.

Campbell recruited 180 volunteers in Newfoundland and set sail for Quebec with three schooners to join Canadian forces. The force of 180 was considered a remarkable number at that time, considering our population and the limited number of Canadian soldiers.

When the Newfoundlanders arrived at the battle scene the Americans were just 70 miles from Quebec and their success seemed imminent. A garrison of 100 soldiers with the still unorganized militia held Quebec, the only place remaining under the British flag. Talk of surrender was in the air when Campbell's Newfoundland forces arrived. Forty soldiers joined the Canadians in the Quebec garrison, and the others moved out with the Canadian forces to prepare for the U.S. invasion. Less than a month later, General Arnold launched the final phase of the planned American invasion of Canada. But by then the Canadians were ready for battle. They easily defeated the Americans, and forced a retreat. It was a great Canadian military victory made possible by Newfoundlanders — one which changed the course of North American history.

Gill — On the morning of August 18, 1704, one of the most outstanding displays of courage in defending a Newfoundland community by a private citizen took place at Bonavista. It was a bright clear sunny morning when several French war vessels, accompanied by Abenaquis Indians in canoes, launched an attack on Bonavista. The inhabitants dreaded the murdering savages even more than they feared the French. Many of them sought refuge in the nearby forest.

But one man showed no fear, and courageously faced the enemy. Newfoundland historian Judge D. W. Prowse described the scene: "Above all this panic and din and craven fear rises the master spirit of the bold New England skipper, Michael Gill. In a moment he is on the alert. The deck is cleared for action; his guns are loaded; his men at their posts ready to give the French a warm reception."

The attackers captured three schooners, taking all on board prisoner. They moved towards Gill's vessel, he opened fire and the battle began. The French, with two heavily-armed vessels, also began their attack.

When the French realized they could not take Gill, they set fire to one of their prizes and cut her lose to drive her upon him. But Gill evaded the attack. The French then set fire to another; Gill evaded this also. When the inhabitants hiding in the hills saw Gill's valiant defiance, they came out of hiding to help Gill in successfully driving the French and their Indian allies away. Gill later became a Judge of the Admiralty Court of Newfoundland and Colonel of the first local militia ever organized here.

Teen Outsmarts Pirates — A 15-year old Carbonear boy once showed great courage in assisting two men in regaining control of a captured cargo ship from French pirates. The vessel was the General Wolfe, owned by the firm of James Kemp of Poole (England) and Carbonear.

The ship was captured by the pirates half-way across the Atlantic, as it travelled from Newfoundland to the Meditteranian to deliver a cargo of fish.

The pirates took the Captain and crew prisoner, but left the mate, one seaman and the 15-year-old Carbonear boy on board. The pirates assigned 10 men to take possession of *the General Wolfe* and to escort her to a French port.

The mate put together a skillful plan to regain control of the ship.

Using a gimlet he bore holes in the companionways, then filled them in with nails. As the ship neared the French coast in broad daylight, the mate gave a signal to the seaman to close the fore-scuttle and place the nails in the holes to secure the French crew when at dinner.

The next step in the plan saw the Carbonear boy seize the Captain's pistol, which the Captain always removed while eating, and toss it to the mate on deck. The mate caught the pistol and pointed it at the helmsman, telling him he would shoot if necessary.

Meanwhile, as the boy tried to escape to the deck, the French Captain seized his legs in an attempt to pull him back. The mate stooped down and seized the boy by the arm, and a tug-o-war between the mate and Captain ensued. The great strength of the mate won out and the boy was rescued.

The French captain was left holding the boy's boots. The

Newfoundland crew of three then took the ship to the English port at Poole, England. At Poole a grateful insurance company presented the trio with a cash award.

Newfoundlanders At Famous Naval Battle — Twenty-two Newfoundlanders took part in the epic naval battle of the War of 1812, fought between the 'Shannon' and the 'Chesapeake'. The Chesapeake was the pride of the American Navy, and had been ordered by Washington to stop British ships from going up the St. Lawrence River.

However, before the vessel could carry out its orders she ran into the Shannon (which had among its crew 22 Newfoundlanders). In 16 minutes flat the pride of the U.S. Navy was reduced to shambles.

The adventure of the 22 Newfoundlanders began on December 5, 1812 from Little Bay, Notre Dame Bay. The men had joined the crew of the 'Brig Duck,' owned by Newman and Company. The ship set out for Portugal with a cargo of fish it intended exchanging for a cargo of wine.

On the 17th day at sea the Duck was captured by the French, its cargo dumped, and then allowed to sail on to Portugal. But the troubles of the Newfoundlanders were far from over. A few days later they were taken prisoners by Captain Plumer of the U.S. Navy. Then a British privateer, under the command of Sir John Sherbrooke, confronted the Americans in battle and rescued them.

Sherbrooke delivered the Newfoundlanders to the famous HMS Shannon which was already short of crew members. The Shannon, stationed at Boston, was under orders to intercept all craft coming out of that port and other New England ports. Meanwhile the Chesapeake had just been re-fitted at Boston, and under the command of Captain Lawrence was unknowingly heading towards a confrontation with the Shannon. When the Chesapeake was sighted by the Shannon, a challenge was issued to the Americans. They accepted.

The Chesapeake had 38 guns while the Shannon had 44, but the Shannon was better handled and her fire was more accurate and deadly. She also had 22 fighting Newfoundlanders on board.

In just 16 minutes the Chesapeake was a wreck and her commander fatally wounded. As Captain Lawrence was carried below he made the famous battle cry that has since been the watchword of the American Navy . . . . "Don't give up the ship." Minutes later Lawrence was dead and the *Chesapeake* crew surrendered.

The official report mentioned the 22 Newfoundlanders, stating they did their work manfully in a celebrated fight. The Newfoundlanders won glory for their country and their employers were given the right to fly the White or Naval Ensign over their Newfoundland establishment.

Chapter XI
Interesting Places and Things

This chapter highlights some of the interesting places in Newfoundland and the colorful stories associated with them, as well as some unusual occurances and things. For example, Father Duffy's Well on the Salmonier Line about thirty miles west of St. John's is a famous watering hole for travellers. There is an interesting story relating to how it got its name.

Father Duffy's Well — Father Duffys Well is actually called after Father Jim Duffy, the first resident parish priest at St. Mary's and one of the most controversial clergymen in New-foundland history. During 1834-1835 Father Duffy led his parishoners in an act of civil disobedience that was interpret-ed by authorities as a rebellion, causing the Governor to send in the military.

The controversy began when the chief clerk employed by the merchant John Martin, a man named Lush, looked out the store window to see Father Duffy and a group of 80 fisher-men demolishing the wharf owned by Martin. They were us-ing axes and burning the wood as it was removed. The clerk ran to the scene to try and stop them. But Father Duffy was not deterred and continued to swing his ax and pile the wood for burning. Some of the men told Lush that the priest had called upon them from the pulpit to follow him in destroying the wharf, either that or face the curse of God and the con-gregation upon them. When the portion of the wharf block-ing an access road was destroyed, Duffy called off his men.

Father Duffy's Well (photo - Jack Fitzgerald).

When Martin returned from St. John's, Father Duffy called on him to remove the rest of the wharf. The priest argued that the beach was the common property of the people of St. Mary's. The fishermen used the area for drying and mending their nets. It also served as part of a road to Riverhead. Martin refused, so Father Duffy once more called on his parishoners to follow him in finishing destruction of the wharf.

This time Martin had Father Duffy charged. He was arrested and taken to Ferryland, where he was released on bail. However, when police came to St. Mary's to take Father Duffy the people armed themselves and wouldn't allow the arrest of the priest. Witnesses refused to acknowledge subpoenas and chased off the police with guns. Bishop Fleming felt Father Duffy had been justified, but advised the people to respect the law. Father Duffy and the ring leaders surrendered to police.

They walked back and forth to St. John's a dozen times, with the case continuously being delayed. The place where they regularly stopped for rest and refreshments was on the Salmonier Line, and became known as Father Duffy's Well.

When the case eventually was heard in court, Father Duffy and his friends were found not guilty.

The Brigus Cave — Many people have seen the Brigus tunnel which was cut over a long distance through solid rock. Legend says it was built by pirates. While less romantic the truth is a good example of the early pioneer spirit in Newfoundland.

During the 19th century, Abram Bartlett found that his property was too inconvenient: the water adjoining it was too shallow to handle his ships. To deal with the problem he purchased from the Percy estate at Brigus a hill dropping almost perpindicularly to the sea. There was no way of using this as a waterfront property unless the solid rock could be penetrated.

Bartlett engaged a Cornish miner named John Hoskins, who came out from England to do the job. Hoskins had a forge built near the construction site to keep the drills sharpened. The only explosive used was gun powder, and it took only four months to build the tunnel.

Dildo and the DO-X — An unplanned and unexpected event in Newfoundland's aviation history took place at Dildo on May 19, 1932. It was an event that captured headlines around the world. Air travel was in its infancy, and the Germans had developed what was at that time the largest flying boat in the world. It was called the DO-X and was designed by Dr. Claudius Dornier.

The aircraft had twelve engines — six pullers and six pushers mounted back to back atop the plane. It was 130 feet long and 31 feet high, with a wing span of 157 feet. The DO-X travelled at a top speed of 150 miles per hour.

Following a series of successful experimental flights in Germany, a trans-Atlantic demonstration flight was planned. This plan took the DO-X from Lake Constance on to Rio de Janiero in Brazil, up the Atlantic Seaboard to New York, and then on to St. John's.

As the giant craft neared Newfoundland it ran into trouble. It ran low on fuel, and changed course for Holyrood. But heavy fog covered Holyrood, forcing the DO-X to make an emergency landing at Dildo Arm. It was 6:45 p.m., and the sudden unexpected appearance of this unusual aircraft in those early days drew surprise and excitement throughout Trinity Bay.

Thousands came from all parts of the Bay to view the world's largest aircraft. S. J. Pretty and Co. of Dildo supplied the craft with fuel and supplies to enable the craft to continue. While the DO-X was at Dildo, Mrs. Ellen George, the postmistress, sent out reports to the world press of the progress of the aircraft.

From Dildo the DO-X moved on to Holyrood. About 1,000 people from St. John's went to Holyrood by train to get a glimpse of the famous flying boat. While it was moored at Holyrood another historical event was taking place at Harbour Grace. That was the landing of Amelia Earhart, the first lady to fly a single-engine plane across the Atlantic.

The experiment showed that the DO-X was too big and expensive to succeed commercially. It was taken out of storage and stored in a Berlin museum, a museum later destroyed by allied bombing during World War II.

Crow's Nest — On the walls of the Crow's Nest in Downtown St. John's, there is a framed floorboard with a nail in it surrounded by a brass ring. The nail was driven in by the skipper of a corvette moored at St. John's Harbour during January, 1942.

To mark the opening of the Crow's Nest on January 27th, 1942, a competition was held to see who could drive a nail into the floor with the least number of blows. The loser was to pay for the drinks. The competition was won by Lt. H. Shadforth, Captain of the Canadian corvette *Spikenard*.

A few days later the *Spikenard* was sunk in the North Atlantic; the Captain and crew went to the bottom with their ship. The floorboard and nail remains on the wall of the Crow's Nest in memory of Captain Shadforth.

Monument at Bannerman Park — There is a monument on display at Bannerman Park dedicated to Father Michael Morris, a 19th century Roman Catholic priest who worked for the orphans of Newfoundland. The devotion and dedication of Father Morris transcended religious boundaries, so that when he became too weak to continue his good works, a Church of England minister stepped in and took over.

Father Morris was a member of the Morris family, famous in Newfoundland history. His brother Frank became a member of the Newfoundland Legislature and later became a Justice of the Supreme Court of Newfoundland. Another brother, Edward Morris, became a member of the Legislature, a cabinet minister, Prime Minister of Newfoundland, and the first native Newfoundlander to be created a peer.

Father Michael was respected across Newfoundland as a great orator. He was a brilliant man and a priest dedicated to improving the lot of the poor, particularly orphans. He worked with clergy of other faiths in helping the poor, becoming a close friend of the noted Newfoundland historian and Church of England minister, Reverend Moses Harvey.

The Franciscan Bishop, J. T. Mullock, had established an orphanage for girls only at Belvedere in St. John's. Times were extremely difficult in Newfoundland at the time, and Father Morris was concerned over the need for a similar institution for boys. He persuaded Bishop Power to buy the Bellevue Hotel at Manuels. He called the new property after his favourite saint — Thomas of Villa Nova. Father Morris never missed an opportunity to promote his orphange at Villa Nova, and thanks to his persuasive speaking abilities help began pouring in.

Sir William Whiteway, then Prime Minister of Newfoundland, gave him a team of Oxen for the farms which Father Morris had set up on Little Bell Island to support the orphanage. Sir Joseph Outerbridge donated Easter lillies to grace the orphanage gardens, and the orphanage was overwhelmed with gifts during its first Christmas in operation.

Along with providing a home for 150 boys, Father Morris offered a variety of training in trades so the boys could find work when they left the orphanage.

When everything seemed to be going well a typhoid epidemic struck. Father Morris remained in residence caring for the sick orphans until he eventually contracted the disease and became confined to bed. A Reverend Colley of the Church of England, Topsail, moved in and continued the work of Father Morris. The boys who died were buried in secret in a wooded area near the orphanage. On August 1, 1889, Father Morris passed away. His body lay in state at the Roman Catholic Cathedral in St. John's for several days. People of all religions lined up to pay their last respects to this saintly priest.

On the day of the funeral, flags flew at half-mast and Water Street stores were closed. The pall-bearers at the funeral included members of the House of Assembly and the Supreme Court, as well as prominent sea captains and merchants.

The public contributed to a fund to erect a monument in memory of Father Morris. This monument consists of a large bronze bust on a stone pedestal and can still be seen on display at Bannerman Park.

St. Clare's Hospital — If it had not been for some gold nuggets from the Klondike, St. Clare's Hospital in St. John's may not have gotten off the ground. St. Clare's Hospital began operation in 1922. Originally it occupied the white house on the corner of St. Clare Avenue and LeMarchant Road, a building that had been previously the home of the Hon. E. M. Jackman. Just before becoming a hospital, it was used as a home for working girls in the city.

Sister Mary Clare English, a Presentation sister, spreaheaded the drive to raise funds to purchase the Jackman home for use as a hospital. The good sister raised most of the money needed for her project by selling a valuable set of prayer beads, which had been given to her family by a family friend.

The prayer beads were made of gold nuggets taken from the Klondike. They were purchased by the Knights of Columbus and later presented to Cardinal Gibbons of Baltimore. Baltimore had a special role in the development of St. Clare's Hospital because it was there that the Sisters of Mercy from Newfoundland received their nurse's training.

St. Clare's Hospital was officially opened on May 21, 1922. From its humble beginnings in a residential home, the hospital has now grown to the point where it can accommodate more than 300 patients. The hospital employs a staff of 800 people.

The Dickinson Monument at Cavendish Square — There is a monument on Cavendish Square near Hotel Newfoundland in St. John's which was erected by the people of the City in memory of Miss Ethel Dickinson, who passed away on Saturday, October 26, 1918.

Miss Dickinson was the victim of a world-wide epidemic

of Spanish Flu that killed millions of people. When that epidemic struck St. John's, Ethel Dickinson was among the first volunteers to provide medical help for the victims. Ethel was the only member of the medical profession in Newfoundlnd to die from the disease. Because of the risk involved in her volunteer work and the tremendous dedication shown by this St. John's nurse, she became an instant Newfoundland heroine.

The epidemic started sweeping the world during the last year of World War I. It was probably caused by the starvation, disease and suffering experienced during the war. Throughout Europe and North America an estimated twenty million people died from the Spanish Flu. Medical authorities noted that the spread of the flu in Newfoundland was checked by the cold weather.

Ethel Dickinson was the niece of city merchant James Pitts, from whom Pitts Memorial Drive bears its name. She was educated at the Methodist College and earned a teaching certificate in Chicago. During World War I she went to Europe as a volunteer in the Auxiliary Division of the Armed Forces. She devoted three years to nursing the sick in France and Flanders. When she returned to St. John's she resumed teaching at Holloway School on Long's Hill.

On October 1, 1918, newspaper headlines flashed this message across front pages: 'Spanish Flu Strikes Town.' Hundreds of cases were reported, mostly among foreign seamen in port. All public gatherings were prohibited and public places closed. Due to overcrowding in city hospitals caused by the epidemic, the King George V Institute was taken over and used as a hospital.

Ethel Dickinson was among the first to work at the Institute; within two weeks she had contacted the flu and died. She had gotten the flu because while accompanying patients to the emergency hospital in the old horse-drawn ambulance, she had left her protective nose and mouth gauze behind. She was 39 years old at the time of her death.

Health regulations at that time required victims of the epidemic to be buried immediately. Ethel Dickinson was buried that same afternoon. Two weeks later the epidemic had passed and the ban on public gathering was lifted. On October 27, 1920, the people of St. John's showed their recognition and appreciation of the unselfish spirit of Ethel Dickinson by unveiling the monument in her memory at Cavendish Square.

The monument is a 14 foot high shaft of Aberdeen granite surmounted by a Celtic Cross. It was unveiled by Governor Alexander Harris.

The Oyster Bed — On March 11, 1907, the Boston *Sunday Herald* carried a news story indicating that a valuable deposit of pearl oysters had been discovered somewhere in Newfoundland. The credibility of the story was assured because the man making the claim was no ordinary person. He was the Reverend Dr. Worchester, Pastor of Emmanuel Church, Boston.

The discovery was made in one of several streams that flow into the Bay of Islands. Reverend Worchester was in Newfoundland to hunt Caribou. He had obtained the services of an indian guide and used a small schooner which he had purchased at Bay of Islands to sail inland.

Describing Worchester's discovery the *Boston Herald* reported that, "Going up into one of the streams with his Indian guide to look for Caribou beds, Dr. Worchester watched the bed of the river closely. Some distance up they discovered an oyster bed and the Indian guide began diving. Time and time again he dived and came up with one or two shells. He had gone down 25 times when he returned to the shore where Dr. Worchester was standing, bringing him two shells which seemed to be pearl bearers. He opened the first one, but it was empty. On opening the second, the sight they beheld almost took their breath away. Reposing snugly in one corner of the shining white shell was a beautiful white pearl."

The *Herald* reported that the Reverend took over 300 pearls and then went onto the interior to hunt caribou. When he returned to Boston he was offered $1500.00 for the pearls.

There was speculation that the *Herald* story was a fraud. One aspect of it which lacked credibility was the paper's claim that Worchester was led to the pearls by the writings of John and Sebastian Cabot. The newspaper explained that the Cabots found pearls in Newfoundland and brought them back to their patron, King Henry VII of England.

A Marine Wonder! — What newspapers around the world were describing as the greatest marine wonder ever devised in the way of a life-boat visited Petty Harbour on Tuesday,

November 15th, 1904. This wonder vessel was called the *Urad* and its home port was Alesund, Norway.

The *Urad* was designed by 22-year-old Captain O. Brude, in response to a public challenge by the French government. The French had offered a big money prize to the mariner who could devise the safest life-boat and give a practical demonstration that the invention was safe.

Brude's invention was a weird-looking contraption. It was egg-shaped — 24 feet long, eight feet wide and eight feet high. The crew was made up of the Captain and three crewmen. To test its ability to survive, Brute set out on a trans-Atlantic trip to Newfoundland and then to New York.

The *Urad* took 100 days to reach Newfoundland. Continuous storms and hurricanes forced the crew to remain inside for the entire trip. The *Urad* travelled several feet below the water and was airtight and waterproof.

After visiting Petty Harbour, the *Urad* went on to St. John's, where thousands of curious spectators visited Bennett's wharf to view the marine wonder. Hundreds paid the ten cent admission fee to board it.

They found the inside pleasant and comfortable. The lockers were upholstered in leather and there were on board some specially designed lifeboats. Newspapers of the time reported that the *Urad* was the most novel boat ever to be seen inside this harbour. After taking on a supply of food and water and undergoing some repairs, the *Urad* set out for New York.

A Communion Set — There is an interesting story in Newfoundland history regarding a communion set donated to the Anglican Community by Prince William Henry. Prince William spent some time in Newfoundland following his appointment as Surrogate Magistrate. Although he showed an interest in local politics, he was careful to act only on the advice of the Governor. He did interfere with the Religious freedom of Roman Catholics, however, and forbade them to worship in the public courthouse at Placentia which they had been using for services.

When the Catholics completed building their first chapel at Placentia an angry Prince William commented, "It demonstrated the prodigious influence the papal priests have over the minds of the weak Irish." The Prince then joined with Protestant merchants in the town in an effort to match the move. They started a drive to raise funds to build an Anglican chapel. At his last Sunday in Placentia the Prince read Divine services at the new chapel, and presented a sterling silver communion set to the congregation.

It consisted of one large silver chalice, one ewer and two patens. It was made during the year 1786 in London by Edward Fennell. The communion set remained in the Bradshaw family at Placentia until 1922, and was then turned over to the Church of England Cathedral in St. John's. It was used in 1974 when the Bishop of London visited St. John's for the 275th anniversary of the St. John's parish.

The Grange — Another fascinating place to visit in Newfoundland is Whitbourne, the site of Sir Robert Bond's estate — once called the Grange. The Grange was one of the most unique estates in all North America. Bond used some of his fortune to transform eight square miles surrounding several beautiful lakes so that it resembled a typical English countryside.

Bond personally supervised the planting of 8,000 imported trees and shrubs, including Norway Spruce, Canadian Maple, Cedars, Swiss Firs, English Oaks, Copper Beech, Scottish Rowan Trees, the Japanese Maple and Siberian Tea Trees. Patches of purple heather can still be seen near the railway tracks at Whitbourne, which was once known as Bond's Cut.

When the project was completed Bond used the estate as a hunting lodge and later expanded it to make it his permanent home. It was Bond who gave Whitbourne its name. He developed it into a village with streets lined with beautiful trees and flowers. On a gentle hill overlooking the village, Bond constructed 'The Grange.'

Prior to being called Whitbourne the community was known as Harbour Grace Junction. While the Grange was being constructed, a fire broke out and Bond's beautifully designed village was destroyed. Bond was not deterred and set out to rebuild the area by clearing the burnt forest and turning it into a model farm.

It was Sir Robert Bond who established the first herd of purebred *Ayrshire* cattle in Newfoundland. Bond gave bull calves to any farmer in the area wanting to improve his own stock. When Bond passed away he left his farm, the Grange, and his entire Whitbourne property to the people of Newfoundland.

In his will he insisted that the farm be maintained as a training centre to benefit the country as a whole. The Government at the time, however, could not afford to meet this condition, so the estate was turned over to Sir Robert's nephew who maintained it for 20 years.

Bond also left some interesting items, which he had kept in his library at the Grange. These included the first ballot box used in Newfoundland, sections of the first trans-atlantic cable, and the first message to cross the Atlantic from Ireland which was given to Bond by Marconi.

Hickman's Harbour — The last home of the Indians on Newfoundland's east coast was at Hickman's Harbour. Two Indian reservations existed there — one called 'Old Tilts' and the second 'Nut Garden'. Over the years excavators have unearthed old Indian pipes and hunting tools. But just how Hickman's Harbour got its name is an interesting story.

In the year 1740 two brothers were born on a vessel crossing the North Atlantic. Their mother died during childbirth and because there was not a clergyman on the ship the father had to christen them. They were named John and Jonathan Hickman.

The Hickman brothers devoted their lives to working at sea and became expert sailors. As a matter of fact, when General Wolfe lead his troops along the St. Lawrence for the Battle of Abraham it was John Hickman who piloted Wolfe's ship.

Jonathan, on the other hand, used his expertise as pilot of the vessel under the command of the famous Captain Cook. It was Cook who charted the first accurate map of Newfoundland. During the year 1762, while charting the Newfoundland coastline, Cook anchored at a harbour which he described as scenic. He named the harbour Hickman's Harbour in honour of his young pilot, who was then 22 years old.

Jonathan later returned to settle at the harbour called after him. He lived there until his death, and his remains are buried near the town hall at Grand Bank.

117

Skin Boot Church — There is a Newfoundland church affectionately referred to by its parishoners as the Skin Boot Church. How this church was built and why it is thus referred to is a fascinating and colorful story.

It's a story that has its beginning in 1920 when there was no church of any size along Newfoundland's north-west coast. The Anglican men and women of the Flower's Cove area got together to discuss the need for a church and to develop means of raising funds for its construction.

Lydia Whalen, a woman living in the area whom the residents called Aunt Lydie, later recalled the interesting episode. She said, "People wasn't so thick then, but all of us that lived on the Strait of Belle Isle figured we needed a Church. Trouble was money wasn't so thick either."

Although times were difficult, the people were fortunate in having as their pastor Reverend J. T. Richards, who was later awarded the Order of the British Empire for his services to the people on Newfoundland's north-west Coast.

Reverend Richards chose to form a cooperative as the best means of getting the church built. At that time Flower's Cove was 500 miles from the nearest road and all the materials had to be brought in by boat or made in the community. For four years 30 men laboured to build the church free of charge. Yet there was still a need for money to buy lumber, altar furnishings, a memorial stained-glass window, nails, bolts, etc. But the parish was broke.

And that's where Aunt Lydie and the Skin Boot idea took root. She suggested that the men go seal-hunting and provide the ladies of the community with the seal-skin so they could make seal-skin boots. Seal-skin boots were popular commodities in the U.S. market at that time.

The idea went over very well. The men caught and tanned hundreds of seals; the Pastor cut out boot patterns; and the women sewed almost 4,000 pairs of boots which Reverend Richards sold at New York and Boston.

The boots were known as Muk-luks and had 84 stitches around the toe and 64 at the heel. The money raised from the project paid for the building of the beautiful Anglican Church at Flower's Cove in less than four years. The proper name of the church is St. Barnabas, but old timers still affectionately call it the Skin Boot Church.

Eskimo Remedy — The most unusual old remedy for an illness that I've come across in researching Newfoundland historical records involved an Eskimo woman's treatment for blood poisoning. While her remedy appears to be rather odd, it certainly worked and it saved the life of a young boy from Trinity Bay.

The young boy was accompanying his father on a fishing trip to the Labrador Coast when the incident occurred. The boy got a hook caught in the palm of his hand. He removed the hook but failed to clean the wound properly. Shortly afterwards his hand swelled and a dark colour began spreading up his arm. The arm had become blood poisoned.

There was no doctor on the coast at that time, but the skipper knew of an old Eskimo woman 40 miles away who possessed the knowledge of ancient Eskimo practices.

The woman viewed the injury and the condition of the boy's hand, then assumed command of the situation with great confidence. She ordered the boy to remove his coat and roll up his sleeves. She then ordered one of the men to go outside and bring back a live hen.

Using a knife, she lanced the wound quickly before the boy could protest. Using the same knife she cut through the back part of the hen's breast bone; then she straightened out the boy's fingers and inserted the whole hand into the body of the hen through the open cut. She then bound the hen tightly over the hand and told the boy to sit still for awhile. The boy's father was surprised and astonished at the result. The dark color in the boy's arm retreated towards the hand. When it disappeared the hen died. The old lady then ordered the men to bury the hen deeply so the dogs couldn't get at it. She noted that if the dogs ate the hen they would become poisoned and die.

Meanwhile, the boy was cured and after a few days he was ready to resume work helping his father.

The Spout — While reviewing old papers at the Provincial Archives I noticed a reference to a James Lawson in an article which stated, "He discovered what he thought was a natural phenomena so unusual and exciting that he felt others would want to share his experiences."

In 1855 a man named John Mullaly described this phenomena as, "One of the greatest natural curiosities in the

Island and perhaps the world.

The phenomena Lawson and Mullaly referred to was a spout situated about three miles south of Petty Harbour. It resembled a giant water fountain that reached as high as 40 feet. It was a well-known landmark and had been mentioned in accounts dealing with Newfoundland from as early as 1689. Several articles about it were published: in the *English Pilot* in 1689, the *Gentleman's Magazine,* in 1754, and in *Edward Chappell's Voyage,* 1818.

Up to the time of the James Lawson visit in 1897 all previous witnesses to the spout had viewed it from sea. Lawson was the first whose curiosity about its source and secret led him to search it out and view it from land.

The overland trek to the Spout was a tough one. Lawson wrote in his diary, "We went through a brulee, which of all things in this world is the most odious to go through. Clouds of charcoal dust rise in suffocating gusts. Your clothes are blackened and rent by shreds of charred unyielding twigs, which retain none of the elasticity of life, but in their deaths are grim and sturdy, prodding the rash intruder and goading him to oaths. Only patience prevails."

In addition to these hardships, Lawson noted that his party was viciously attacked by black flies. Eventually they reached a point where they heard the thunder of the Spout and climbing up a cliff they were able to see it.

Lawson was impressed by the view, but the others from St. John's felt it was a waste of time and vowed never to return. Lawson described the Spout thus: "The vent of the Spout is a couple of feet in diameter; and in the intervals that occur between the spoutings of the waters, it is an easy enough matter to approach and look down into the funnel. Thirty yards away is an open cave to the Atlantic. The Spout is 30 feet above sea level." There is a legend that claims the Spout is the hiding place of pirates treasure.

The Logy Bay Spa — A discovery during the 1840's at Logy Bay by a Dr. Kielley lead to speculation that tourists from all over the world would converge on the community to benefit from the findings. Kielley's discovery was a genuine 'Spa', which was of special interest to people suffering from chronic Rhumatism, diseases of the skin, indigestion, and a variety of·

other ailments.

Kielley, a St. John's-based doctor, discovered the spa while making house calls in the Logy Bay area. He was supported by Newfoundland Governor Thomas Cochrane in his enthusiasm and belief in the spa's curing qualities. He sent a sample of the water from the spa to the British analyst Sir William Herepath at Bristol, who was a friend of Governor Cochrane. Herepath gave the sampling a very high rating, noting it contained nine chemical ingredients. He said it was of a higher quality than the famous King's Bath Spa located at Bath, England.

Newfoundland authorities considered turning the area into a tourist attraction — but the idea lost momentum. The spa was never developed.

Gilbert's Boat — When Old Day's Pond at Bonavista Bay was drained in 1926, a group of fishermen unearthed an object from the bottom which had a connection with one of the best-known events in Newfoundland history. Unfortunately, the men had no idea of its value. They destroyed it.

The men had discovered the remains of a black-oak lifeboat, of the type used by the English during the reign of Queen Elizabeth I. The timbers and planking were still intact and the measurements and identifying material were easily obtainable.

The craft had a brass disk fixed to it, showing the date 1583. On the disk was displayed an emblem, the heads of a double eagle with the letter G in between. A French coin from the time of Louis XIII of France was found jammed in the boat timber.

The workmen were not impressed by their find. They simply broke up the wood and divided it among themselves. Some dried the wood and used it as firewood. The others made oak walking sticks.

The brass disk, meanwhile passed from family to family. In 1930 it fell into the hands of the Anglican clergyman, Reverend Canon Boyle. Boyle was curious as to where the boat came from and what the emblem represented. Through study and research he learned the boat had been 25 feet long and the date on the plate coincided with the year Sir Humphrey Gilbert had claimed Newfoundland. Gilbert was the only one known to hold a patent for Newfoundland at that period. Boyle was satisfied that the emblem was Sir Humphrey Gilbert's, and the boat had once belonged to him.

The Plaque — There is a plaque on display at the St. Anthony Hospital dedicated to the memory of three dogs. Their names were Moody, Watch and Spy. The dogs were owned by Sir Wilfred Grenfell and are memorialized because the famous doctor had to kill them in order to stay alive.

Grenfell's brush with death took place on April 21, 1908. He was travelling alone by dog team to Brent's Island, 60 miles South of St. Anthony, to visit a sick boy. While crossing a frozen bay, heavy offshore winds moved the ice, causing it to break up. The ice was being tossed around and slowly drifting out to sea when his sled, which carried blankets, food and medical supplies, slipped into the waters. Grenfell and his three dogs were left stranded on an ice pan, 10 feet by 8.

Grenfell prayed for a miracle. To avoid freezing he cut off his long moccasins down to his feet, then slit the legs of these and made a jacket which protected him from the wind, at least from the waist down.

In desperation he was forced to kill three of his dogs, using the furs to cover himself. He also used the carcases to rest on and avoid getting wet. The legs of the dogs he used to make a flagpost so he could signal for help.

Meanwhile, unknown to Grenfell, he had been spotted by an old fishermen who was scouring the bay with binoculars in search of seals. The old man told George Andrews and four other fishermen. The five waited until daylight and then set out to rescue Grenfell.

It was a difficult task with the broken ice being tossed around in the sea. Yet they made it to Grenfell and returned him safely to shore.

Sir Wilfred showed his appreciation to his rescuers by presenting each one with a watch. Inscribed on back of each was the date April 21, 1908, the date of the rescue. He had a plaque placed at the Hospital to memorialize the three dogs for the role they played in his survival.

Unusual Names — Tourists visiting Newfoundland are sometimes as fascinated by the strange and unusual names of some of our communities as they are by the attractiveness of our province's rugged beauty. In 1904 the Newfoundland Government changed some of the more unusual names; yet they continue to add color and interest to our history.

For example, St. Chad's, Bonavista Bay, was originally called Damn The Bell Cove — and some pronounced it as Damnable Cove.

The name originated during the 1740's when a private vessel raced along the Bonavista coastline followed by a British man-o-war. The pirates slipped into a hidden harbour to escape the British. The British followed them, circled the harbour, but were unable to find them. Just as they were leaving the harbour, one of the pirates tripped over the ship's bell, causing it to ring and drawing the attention of the British. The pirate captain shouted, "Damn the bell". They were captured and taken as prisoners to England where several of them were hanged. The harbour continued to be called Damn The Bell Harbour until 1869, when a clergyman renamed it St. Chad's.

Job's Cove, Conception Bay, was originally known as Devil's Cove. This name offended the inhabitants and they petitioned the Government to change the name to Job's Cove.

When a limestone quarry started at Jack of Club's Cove in 1911, the people there petitioned the Government to change its name and it became known as Aquathuna. Aquathuna was a Beothuck name meaning grindstone.

Curling at the Bay of Islands was named after Reverend J. J. Curling, an Anglican priest. It was first called Birchy Cove. Dunfield, Trinity Bay, was originally known as Cuckold's Cove, and Lumsden was known as Cat Cove.

O'Regan, Bay St. George, is named after Father Charles O'Regan, a Roman Catholic priest who lost his life in a shipwreck while visiting Rose Blanch in 1901. It was previously called Backlands.

Grand River Gut became known as Searstown. St. Bride's was first called Distress; Marysvale, Turk's Gut; Fairhaven, Famish Gut; Placentia Bay, Bread and Cheeze; Pelley's Island, Bumble Bee Bight; Bay D'Espoir, Cock n Hen Cove; St. Barbe Coast, Dog Pen; Bonavista Bay, Fair and False; Trinity Bay, God Almighty Cove; and Red Island, Hole in the Wall.

Nick's Nose Cove had its name changed to Notre Dame

Bay; Pick Eyes became Port de Grave and Stepaside was renamed Burin.

Kelly's Island — Kelly's Island in Conception Bay is now deserted, inhabited only by large Arctic Hares. The island got its name from the pirate Captain Alphonse Kelly, who died on the island leaving a treasure buried in a secret location.

The stones used to build the Roman Catholic Basilica, the Court House at Harbour Grace and Mercy Convent in St. John's, were taken from Kelly's Island. There is a large anchor still embedded in the beach by the lagoon where Kelly operated a careenage and headquarters.

The Island was privately owned. On April 6th, 1909, Alice G. Fawcette, administrator of the Estate of Colonel Morris J. Fawcette, sold all rights and title to the estate (consisting of 120 acres of land) at Kelly's Island to Gustav H. Dickinson of St. John's for $250.00. During 1890 a wedding took place on the island between Sam Porter of Port de Grave and Jane Bussey, a resident of Kelly's Island.

Late one evening during 1901 a strange occurance on the island renewed interest in the stories of buried treasure. On that day a British Naval Lieutenant stepped off the train at Topsail and engaged a local fishermen there to take him out to the island. When they reached it, the Officer ordered the fishermen to wait on the beach while he disappeared into the darkness. An hour later he returned carrying a large boiler which he stored in the boat. The two then headed back for the mainland. As the boat approached Topsail the Lieutenant pulled a gun and shouted, "No, you don't!" He pointed it at the startled fishermen. "Set me ashore over there," he ordered. And he pointed towards an uninhabited section of the shore. When they arrived on shore, the Lieutenant tossed him a ten-dollar bill, grabbed the boiler, and disappeared into the darkness without a word. He was never seen again.

The fishermen located some old Spanish gold doubloons in the bottom of his boat the next day. The incident convinced the local people that there was truth to the stories of pirate treasure on the island.

The Tough Duff — Around the year 1904 the Newfoundland sealing vessel *Terra Nova* delivered a cargo of seal skins to Scotland. Following the delivery of the cargo, while the crew were in the process of giving the entire ship a thorough cleaning, they discovered an item at the top of a shelf in the pantry which completely puzzled them.

All day long the crew tried to determine what the item was. Throughout all the guessing the cook, John Grant, kept silent. They felt certain at least of one thing: the item was a piece of quality wood. Grant smiled, emptied his pipe and walked out of the room without commenting.

The others, still curious, sought out some Scotish ship-builders on shore, to solicit their help in identifying the mystery object. The experts sawed it in half and identified it as one of several kinds of hardwood. One Scotsman suggested it was greenheart or lihnium vitae. But even the experts couldn't agree.

When the Terra Nova set sail from Scotland the object was still a mystery. Then Grant stepped forward and offered to solve the mystery. While his mates were skeptical, they listened attentively to his explanation.

Grant was known among Newfoundland sealers for the great figgy duffs he made. He made these from water, flour and molasses, then boiled them in a cotton bag. Two years earlier, after supplying the crew with a meal of duff he had one serving left over which was about the size of a small cabbage. He stored it in the galley on a shelf. Gradually the heat hardened the duff, and Grant forgot it was there. The mystery object turned out to be a two-year-old figgy duff made by Grant.

Chapter 12
Newfoundland Heroes

"Congressional Medal of Honour Winner" — The American Congressional Medal of Honor was awarded in 1877 to Michael McCarthy of St. John's for his outstanding heroic conduct during an Indian uprising in Idaho. McCarthy was born in St. John's on April 19, 1847. By 1877 he was a citizen of the United States and a Sergeant in the First U.S. Cavalry. He was also the veteran of many battles, but none were so fierce as the savage battle his troop waged with the Nez Perces Indians of Idaho.

This tribe had been on friendly terms with the white population. They had always treated their white neighbours with hospitality and generosity. While the white men acted hostilly towards the Nez Perces out of fear or general prejudice, the Indians remained quiet and peaceable, attending strictly to their own affairs.

The Nez Perces had been moved from reservation to reservation to accommodate the expansion of Idaho's white population. A treaty between the Indians and Washington had given the Nez Perces possession of the Wallowas Valley. The Indians seemed content with this settlement, until a group of white settlers moved into the valley. They claimed land which had been given by treaty to the Indians.

At first the Indians tried to settle the land dispute peacefully. They argued that since this land had been given them by treaty as part of the reservation, they were the rightful owners. The white settlers sent a delegation to Washington and succeeded in persuading the Government of the importance of their having ownership of the disputed land. Washignton

127

gave in to the settlers' demands and sent a military force to back them up.

The Nez Perces Chief, Looking Glass, held a council with other tribe leaders and the decision was made to respect the white man's law. They agreed they would move their tribe to another site. While the Indians prepared to move, some white settlers became impatient and began to annoy them. A settler then deliberately shot and killed a Nez Perces. This shot ignited the smouldering discontent among the tribe members and sparked an open rebellion. The peaceful Nez Perces suddenly became as violent and valiant a foe as was ever encountered by an American soldier.

The Indians first act of aggression was the revenge killing of the brother of the white settler who had killed their fellow tribe member. This caused fear and anger among the settlers, who feared a massacre. The settlers successfully obtained military support from Washington. Meanwhile the Indians left their reservation and were heading northeast, towards Montana. They were pursued by the U.S. Cavalry.

Army General Howard issued the following orders to Captain Perry of the First U.S. Cavalry; "Get to the scene quickly, take away from the Indians their loot and chase them back to the reservation." Captain Perry did not realize the Nez Perces determination to fight the white man if necessary. Perry felt a show of force would be enough to bring the tribe into submission. Consequently, when his 90-man party left Fort Lapwai they were poorly equipped. They had only 40 rounds of ammunition for their single carbine and twelve bullets for each pistol.

After riding for 24 hours, with the troops near exhaustion, Perry's men caught up with Chief 'Looking Glass' at White Bird Canyon. Captain Perry was caught by surprise: the Indians occupied a strong position and indicated that they had no intention of surrendering. A battle was inevitable.

The result was the battle of White Bird Canyon on June 17, 1877. It saw the defeat of the U.S. Cavalry and Sergeant McCarthy being awarded the U.S. Congressional Medal of Honor.

The Nez Perces outnumbered the U.S. troops eight to one. In addition, they were in an unassailable position. Captain Perry noticed that to his right was an elevation of rocky ground. He ordered Sergeant McCarthy with a detail of six men to take that position and hold it at all costs.

U.S. congressional records described the battle: "Now the fight began. The Indians broke forth, yelling, screaming, filling the air with hideous howels and showers of bullets. As soon as this rush was made it looked as though hades itself had been turned loose. Eight citizens, settlers who had been most loud in their denunciation of the Nez Perces and their demands for vengeance, took to their heels and ran away as fast as they could. The soldiers too were not prepared to meet this furious and awe-inspiring onslaught and wavered. Soon most of the men of 'F' troop were hurrying to the rear.

"Captain Perry, doubting the advisability of the defence, ordered a general retreat. Captain Trimble felt Perry was making a big mistake. He galloped to the Commanding Officer and pleaded with him to recall the order. He asked, 'What is to become of McCarthy and his men. They are in a strong position. If we reinforce him and hold ground there, we shall check the attack.' Captain Perry was impressed with Trimble's spirit and argument. He reversed his order. Trimble personally led the men back into battle, but there was still confusion in the ranks.

McCarthy noticed the cavalry's change in tactics and hurridly rode from his position to assist his Captain in steadying the men. Once the attack was properly organized, he joined his faithful six men at the former post. The new burst of courage and enthusiastic fighting by the Calvalry was not enough to withstand the onslaught of the overwhelming Nez Perces force. Congressional records describe the scene: "Once more the troops retreated before the exultant Nez Perces, galloping to some hills which promised protection about a mile away. Their retreat was much faster than the Indians were able to follow. This second retreat left McCarthy and his detail in a serious plight. Completely surrounded by savages he nobly and heroically held his position against the storming foe.

"The struggle was observed by his comrades on the hills, who followed every phase of it with anticipations of awe and terror. Closer and closer the Indians drew their circle around the gallant little band. One could now see them shoot, strike or club the foremost of the redskins. Now it was a hand-to-hand fight. Now McCarthy and his comrades could no longer be seen. They were swallowed up by the hordes of screaming Indians. The soldiers who were watching from the hill and witnessing the hand to hand battle turned away, sickened by the sight. But again, the figure of McCarthy and his little party sprung up in the middle of the tribe. The gallant little band was cutting its way through the hostilities."

Although the odds were against him, Lieutenant W. R. Parnell, inspired by the sight of McCarthy's courage, led a detachment of cavalry to help the battling Newfoundlander. McCarthy fought his way through the Indians and joined up with Parnell and his men. Two of McCarthy's men, however, died bravely during the brief but savage ride.

Reinforced by Parnell's detachment, the little group made another stand against the Nez Perces, but in vain. The Indian force was so overwhelming that Parnell ordered a retreat. McCarthy seemed to ignore or not to hear the retreat order, and continued to fight without any regard for his own personal safety. He helped a wounded comrade who fell off his horse from being captured by the savages. He encouraged and tried to control the men who had remained with him to fight. When his horse was shot from under him, he quickly mounted another and slowly guided his men back to the rest of his company. During this retreat his horse was shot from under him again; and in the chaos that followed the courageous sergeant was separated from his comrades.

McCarthy didn't panic. He saw a clump of bushes behind the Indians, and made a dash on foot for them, crawling into the bushes as fast and as far as he could. From his hiding place he could hear the shooting and see the victorious Indians ride by. He could also see his comrades running for their lives. McCarthy was filled with anger and resentment because he could not do anything to help them. He realized the battle was over and his troop had been humiliated by the Nez Perces.

Nearby lay the body of his close friend; but before he had a chance to hide it, a number of squaws came up and began mutilating the body and removing the dead man's clothing. McCarthy realized that his own boots were sticking out of the bushes. Realizing that the squaws had already seen the boots, he slipped out of them and withdrew further into the woods. This was enough to fool the Indian women, who believed some soldier must have left them during a quick retreat.

After many hours of patient waiting, McCarthy, bootless and with an empty gun, made his escape by crawling down the bed of the creek and finally reaching the timbered mountains some miles away. From there he wondered over rough territory which caused agonizing pain to his feet. The New foundland cavalry man hid by day, and travelled by night, living on the scant rations he had with him. After continuous hardships, he arrived at his camp at Mount Idaho, thoroughly exhausted. His safe return caused great rejoicing.

The leaders of the Cavalry carefully documented McCarthy's behavior and forwarded their recommendation to Washington that he be awarded the Congressional Medal of Honour. He was also appointed Captain of the Presidential Guard at the American Whitehouse. The story of McCarthy is carefully preserved in records at the U.S. Congressional Library at Washington, D.C.

"They Faced Death For 64 Hours" — Cold Atlantic waters, below freezing temperatures and 64 hours of exposure to winter weather without food were not enough to defeat George Piercey, a lighthouse keeper at Green Island, Fortune Bay. Piercey overcame all these hardships and in the process saved another man's life, earning himself a Royal Humane Society Medal for heroism.

At the time of Piercey's struggle with death he was a cook on the 30-ton schooner *B.C. McGrath*. Others onboard included Captain Alford, the ships owner, and John Woodland a mate.

Early in December, 1934, the schooner left its home port of Fortune, for Bay D'Espoir, to pick up a cargo of drums for Miquelon. This part of the voyage proceeded without any trouble. When the craft left Miquelon to return home on December 20th, the crew little suspected that before the day was out the *B.C. McGrath* would be on the bottom of the Atlantic and one of the three crewmen would be dead.

The 'Schooner' left Miquelon at 4:00 A.M. in favourable weather. It had sailed only five miles when suddenly the wind changed from westerly to south-westerly. With the change in winds came heavy seas and fearing a storm Captain Alford decided to change course and head for Pass Island. Meanwhile, the winds increased to gale force, followed by a blinding snow storm.

The schooner would have made it to safety that day had the unexpected not occurred. About a mile from Pass Island, a heavy wave struck the vessel and carried away the rudder.

The storm was now so intense that the vessel seemed to be swallowed up in darkness and with the rudder gone the little craft started to drift towards the rocks. In an effort to regain control, Captain Alford threw a cable over the quarter to act as a rudder. But this effort proved useless. The rolling sea took the small craft nearer and nearer to land. She cleared Pass Island and shot out into the mouth of the tickle. A few minutes later the seas swept the vessel to within 50 yards of the mainland, where she grounded close to a small rock. The continuous pounding of the craft by the high seas made it obvious to the Captain that the craft would soon break up.

There was no lifeboat on the craft, and the only hope of escaping a watery grave was by jumping from the bow to the rocks, a distance of about four feet. The heavy blowing snow made it impossible to judge the distance from the mainland. The Captain discussed the desperate situation with his two crewmembers and decided to abandon ship. All three made the rock safely. But they were up to their waists in water; the sea swept over it and made it impossible for them to keep a footing. The Skipper remarked "It would be no good attempting to swim ashore as we would only drown. "The ship's mate could not swim, and Piercey was not a strong swimmer.

Captain Alford suggested they would have a chance of making it if they could manage to secure a line. Piercey volunteered to carry out the suggestion. Since the trio had not taken any line with them, Piercey had to go back on to the abandoned ship, which was threatening to break up at any minute. After a few minutes he was back on the rock with a heavy rope. Although Piercey was cold and frightened, he again volunteered to plunge into the frigid Atlantic and swim to shore in order to secure the line.

He struggled with the rolling sea and safely made his way to shore. With the other end of the rope tied around Woodland, the non-swimmer of the group, Piercey signaled to him to jump into the water. Woodland whispered a short prayer. Realizing that if he didn't take this chance he would certainly die, he made the plunge — and Piercey began pulling him to shore as fast as he could. The mate made it to shore safely. Piercey then gave one end of the rope to Woodland, and taking the other end dived again into the icy waters to bring the line to the Captain. The Captain held the line; Piercey again went into the waters, going along the line hand over hand un til he reached shore. Captain Alford tied the rope around his waist, and his two companions pulled him to safety. Just as the Captain was being pulled out of the waters, the vessel began breaking up.

The men's ordeal was not yet over. As a matter of fact, they had another 60 hours of staring death in the face. Their first struggle was their effort to get off the beach and head for civilization. To do this they had to scale a perpindicular cliff which was slippery and snow covered. Faced with no other choice, they started the climb step by step, helping each other along the way.

Once they reached the top they didn't stop. The trio continued walking in the waste-deep snow, but there was one consolation: the storm seemed to be subsiding. By noon that day they received a glimmer of hope when they spotted a hut which looked like a small house at Beck's Bay. Fate had played a cruel trick on the men. What they thought and hoped was a house turned out to be an ice house. They took refuge inside for the night. At least they had protection from the cold winter winds.

Shortly after entering the house, Woodland collapsed from exhaustion. Even though artificial respiration was given, he grew worse; by early next morning he was dead.

Alford and Piercey had little time to mourn. They knew that if they hoped to survive themselves they must get to civilization as quickly as possible. At the break of dawn the two set out for Grole, Hermitage Bay, which was about one and a half hours' walk away. During their trek the two lost their way and wandered through fields and forest. They were near exhaustion, cold and hungry, but they pushed on. Each step now became a tremendous effort. They prayed for God's help and offered each other encouraging words. The ordeal took its toll on Captain Alford. With seemingly no end to this struggle for survival, the Captain finally lay down in the snow and resigned himself to death.

Piercey, however, was not yet willing to give up. He refused to go on alone and encouraged Alford to get back on his feet and try again. The Captain got up, and Piercey put his arm around him to help him along. A few hours later they reached a cabin where they rested for the night.

The next morning Piercey again persuaded the Captain to come with him to try and find Grole. It was now December 23rd. When Piercey saw two men approaching from the dis-

133

tance he knew his prayers had been answered. The men assisted Piercey and Alford to their homes and offered them food and warm clothing. This was their first taste of food in 64 hours. When they were told of the tragic loss of the *B.C. McGrath,* the rescuers organized a group of twenty men and set out to recover the body of Woodland. Alford and Piercey were now only a half mile from Grole.

On Christmas Eve Alford and Piercey, along with their deceased friend Woodland, were put on board the S.S. *Cape Agulhas* and taken to Fortune. They were home in time to spend Christmas with their families. On Boxing Day Piercey suddenly took ill. He was taken to hospital, where he spent nearly a month recovering. He recovered and later became the lightkeeper at Green Island, Fortune Bay.

Piercey was also a veteran of World War I, having served in France with 'D' Company of the Newfoundland Regiment. On May 8, 1936, George Pircey was awarded the Royal Humane Society's Bronze Medal and a certificate for bravery in recognition of his heroic deeds.

A Hero From the Calypso — On the morning of November 25, 1902, William Cullen left his home on Queen Street in St. John's to attend a training session on the Calypso, a naval-training vessel anchored in the Harbour. Before the day was over he would be fighting to save his own life and the life of a five-year-old St. John's boy.

Cullen was a member of the Royal Navy Reserve. His group had been assigned to the Calypso for special trianing. On that cold November day, Cullen and two other Reserve members were ordered by their Commanding Officer to go over to the Pitt's Premises near Harvey's Wharf and pick up some ship's supplies. They were given a large row boat from the Calypso to use. As they were nearing completion of their task, Cullen, carrying a large mattress on his back, heard the alarming cry of "Boy overboard."

Five-year-old Willie Earles had been playing on the wharf that afternoon. The medium-high winds blowing down the harbour were causing the harbour waters to splash hard against the wharf. Young Earles stepped closer to the edge to get a better look, and he suddenly found himself tumbling head over heels into the dark cold waters. As Earles disappeared into the darkness, a heavy wave washed in; as it receeded it took the little boy farther away from the pier.

Cullen was all rigged out for the cold winter weather. He was wearing his regulation winter navy uniform and a pair of heavy high sea boots. Without any consideration for his own safety, and making no effort to remove any of his clothing, Cullen dropped the mattress and ran to the edge of the wharf. He could see Earles in the water. Without hesitation, the Naval Reserve officer jumped into the icy waters and began swimming towards the drowning boy.

Cullen was a strong swimmer and in a few strokes he was at the boy's side. When he tried to put his right arm around the boy, Earles panicked and grasped Cullen's arm and leg in a death grip. The combination of chilling water, heavy clothing, and the boy's strong grasp nearly exhausted Cullen. He tried to shake off the boy's grasp which was pulling them both under. His friends on shore had tossed a rescue line to him which was a few feet away. Struggling to keep himself and the boy above water, Cullen made it to the rope. At the same time he broke the boy's grip. Then he put his right arm around the boy's neck, and with the other arm seized the life line. His friends on shore pulled the two near enough the pier for some men in a rowboat to pull them out of the water. At first it seemed as if the boy was dead, but he soon came around.

Petty Officer Wilcox, who was in charge of the crew from the Calypso, reported the heroic deed to Captain Walker, who documented the incident and forwarded his report to the Royal Humane Society. On September 30, 1903, the Society presented its medal of heroism to William Cullen. The presentation took place on the HMS *Charybois* and was made in the presence of all the ships in port by Lady Montgomery, wife of the Commodore of the British North American fleet. Cullen accepted the honour with thanks and red cheeks.

William Earle, the five-year-old who almost lost his life in St. John's Harbour, is shown here sixty-years later at his home at the Battery.

Dynamite-Hero — When the Union Forces of U.S. President Abraham Lincoln developed a plan to close the final Confederate port on the Eastern Seaboard, a young Newfoundlander was to play a heroic part in the daring and dangerous plan. Not only would John Neil be one of the eight men involved in the top-secret operation, but he would also earn distinction for himself and bring honour to Newfoundland by being awarded the Congressional Medal of Honour.

According to records of the U.S. Congressional Library: "The splendid energy of the Union Navy in blockading a seacoast of nearly 3,500 miles had such effect that a year after the commencement of the war there were practically only two ports open along the whole hostile coast — Charleston, South Carolina and Wilmington, North Carolina. They were the channels through which the Confederates, by means of daring and fast blockade runners, communicated with the outer world and obtained all the supplies and provisions they wanted in exchange for their cotton. It was impossible for the Navy to close those two places at the time with the sea forces available and without the co-operation of the army; but the army had its hands full just then in other parts of the theatre of war."

When the Federal Navy eventually succeeded in blocking Charleston, the Confederates fell back to Wilmington, their new base of operations. On September 22, 1864, Rear Admiral Porter was assigned to command the North Atlantic Squadron of the Federal navy. The main objective of his naval strategy was to close the only port now left open to the Confederates — Wilmington. If he succeeded, his achievement would hasten the end of the Civil War.

At the mouth of Wilmington Harbour was Fort Fisher, with seventy-five guns mounted behind heavy earthworks. Most of the ships in the Federal Navy were wooden, which made a direct attack by the Squadron a risky proposition. An answer to Porter's dilemma came on November 1st, 1865, when General Butler boarded the admiral's flagship with a daring plan to knock out the guns at Fort Fisher. Butler's plan called for 150 tons of gun-powder being placed aboard a vessel, bringing the vessel as close to the fort as possible, and then blowing up the vessel. The General suggested that the tremendous shock would level the fort or at least dismount the guns.

This plan was thoroughly investigated by competent military strategists, who reported back that it was perfectly feasible providing the whole cargo of 150 tons could be detonated simultanously. That was enough for Admiral Porter; he immediately telegraphed the Navy Ordnance Department for the powder. In his haste, Porter wrote two zeros too many in the telegram, and when Captain wise of the Ordnance Department read it he shook his head in amazement at the request for 15,000 tons of powder. He telegraphed Porter asking "Why do you not ask us to send you Niagara and Vesuvias down there. That would satisfy you."

Meanwhile, Porter was busy putting the plan together. He secured the *Louisiana,* an old vessel, to serve as the powder boat. The powder was stored in bags aboard the vessel. All Porter needed now was a crew of volunteers to sail the boat to its dangerous destination.

In Beaufort, North Carolina, the powder boat was fitted out for her perilous trip, fuses being carefully laid to assure the simultaneous explosion, to be caused by candles and some system of clock work.

With the *Louisana* now in readiness, Porter sought out volunteers for the mission. The 75 guns at the entrance to Wilmington Harbour meant the mission would be in great danger once the vessel came within firing distance of the fort. The Admiral succeeded in getting eight men to volunteer for the dangerous task. One of the first to volunteer was quartergunner John Neil, a Newfoundlander. Neil was a crewmember of the *Agawam.*

On the night of December 23rd the plan went into operation. Admiral Porter made one final change in his plan just before it got underway. In spite of expert opinion, Porter was skeptical over the clockwork and candle arrangement. He suggested that it would be wise to light some pine-knots in the cabin before leaving the boats, so as to make sure of the explosion.

The eight courageous men then set out for the target under the command of commander Rhind. There was a great deal of tension as the ship slipped into the harbour beneath the enemy guns: they could be blown to kingdom come if detected. After what seemed like an eternity to Rhind and his men, they finally got the vessel into position beneath their target.

The men acted swiftly in lighting the candles and pine knots. The candles and the clock-work were to explode the ship in an hour and a half. Having completed their part of the plan, Rhind and his men slipped into the water and began their treacherous swim to a small boat anchored nearby out of sight of the Fort.

The explosion did not occur as planned. After two hours passed there was an explosion. As Admiral Porter had feared the candle work had failed, but the pine knots did the trick. But, they did not cause a simultaneous explosion; consequently, the enterprise failed.

The explosion was terrific and caused extensive damage to the Fort. The next day Porter received a first-hand account of what happened when four Confederate deserters boarded his ship, the *Malvern*.

The heroic deed of the eight men was followed by a heavy naval bombardment of Wilmington. The shot and shell crashed into Fort Fisher at the rate of 115 per minute. An hour and a half into the battle the guns in the fort were silenced. Not a single naval man was injured. The only casualties on the Federal side resulted from exploding Parrott guns and within days the Confederate forces had surrendered. The strategic Fort Fisher, along with some nearby inlets, were now in the hands of the Federal Forces. The President of the United States was elated.

Out of the thousands of troops involved in that Battle at Fort Fisher only a handful of men earned the coveted Congressional Medal of honour. Newfoundlander John Neil was one of them.

Bibliography

Books:

Encyclopedia of Newfoundland, Vols. I and II; Joseph R. Smallwood, Newfoundland Book Publishers (1967 Ltd.).

Books of Newfoundland, Vols. 1-4; Joseph R. Smallwood, Newfoundland Book Publishers, 1937, 1967, 1975.

Newfoundland Miscellany, Joseph R. Smallwood, Newfoundland Book Publishers (1967) Ltd.

Discourse and Discovery, Sir Richard Whitbourne, London, Felix Kyngston, 1620.

Newfoundland in 1897; Moses Harvye, London, Samson Low, Marston, 1897.

The Textbook of Newfoundland History, Moses Harvey, London, Colins, 1890.

Captain John Mason, Dean John Ward, Boston, the Prince Society, 1887.

History of Newfoundland and Labrador, Hon. Fredrick W. Rowe, McGraw Hill, Ryerson Ltd., Toronto, 1980.

A History of the Island of Newfoundland, Lewis Anspach, London, Sherwood, Gilbert, Piper, 1827.

Newfoundland In 1842, Sir Richard Bonnycastle, London, Henry Colburn, 1842.

In Northern Labrador, William Cabot, London, John Murray, 1912.

The Church of England In Newfoundland, Thomas Collett, correspondence, St. John's, 1853.

Sir Wilfred Grenfell, Winnifred M. Combe, Linds-Lutterworth Press, 1950.

History of Newfoundland, D. Prowse, Who Was Who In America, (1943-1955)

Newspapers

Daily News, 1900-1957; Daily Review, St. John's, 1900-1908; Evening Chronicle, St. John's, 1910-1912; Evening Telegram, St. John's, 1892-1940; Newfoundland Gazette, 1850-1892; Newfoundland Patriot, St. John's, 1850-1870;

Newfoundland Stories and Ballads, 1954-1960; The Newfoundlander, St. John's, 1950; Public Ledger, St. John's, 1820-1850; Royal Gazette, St. John's, 1807-1860; Twillingate Sun, Twillingate, 1880-1890; Western Star, Corner Brook, 1903-1904.

Records:

Individual Files, community files and special interest files; Newfoundland Historical Society, St. John's.

Official Documents:

The Record of The Judicial Proceedings held by His Majesty's Justices of the Peace for the District of Trinity In The Island of Newfoundland 1753-1774.

Nfld. Archives, Colonial Secretary's Letter, GN 2/1/2, Vol. 2, 1752-1759.